The Pinkerton Agency: The History of Allan Pinkerton and A Major Private Detective Organization

By Charles River Editors

An 1884 depiction of Pinkerton agents escorting strikebreakers in Ohio

About Charles River Editors

Charles River Editors is a boutique digital publishing company, specializing in bringing history back to life with educational and engaging books on a wide range of topics. Keep up to date with our new and free offerings with this 5 second sign up on our weekly mailing list, and visit Our Kindle Author Page to see other recently published Kindle titles.

We make these books for you and always want to know our readers' opinions, so we encourage you to leave reviews and look forward to publishing new and exciting titles each week.

Introduction

THE HOMESTEAD RIOT—DRAWN BY W. P. SNYDER AFTER A PHOTOGRAPH BY DABBS, PITTSBURG.—[SEE PAGE 829.]
THE PINKERTON MEN LEAVING THE BARGES AFTER THE SURRENDER.

A depiction of Pinkerton agents during the Homestead Strike

The Pinkerton Agency

"By the mid-1850s a few businessmen saw the need for greater control over their employees; their solution was to sponsor a private detective system. In February 1855, Allan Pinkerton, after consulting with six midwestern railroads, created such an agency in Chicago." - Frank Morn, historian

The private detective looms large in popular culture, both in the United States and around the world. From Sir Arthur Conan Doyle's Sherlock Holmes to Raymond Chandler's Philip Marlowe and even 1980s' Thomas Magnum, private detectives have been a staple of novels, movies, and television shows for well over a century. The loner for hire, trying to solve a mystery or right a wrong using nothing but their own brain (in Holmes' case), brawn (in Marlowe's case), or boy next door charm (in Magnum's case), is deeply rooted in the collective psyche of generations of men and women. The fact that today's private detective is more likely to be chasing a cheating spouse than tracking down a desperate criminal is beside the point.

Holmes, Marlowe, and Magnum owe their existence to the first private detective—and if not the first, certainly in the United States the most famous. The name Allan Pinkerton was for decades synonymous with private detective; indeed, the work "Pinkerton" was generally used for any private detective whether or not they were associated with the Pinkerton National Detective Agency. The all-seeing eye that served as the symbol of his company and the slogan—"We Never Sleep"—projected an image of a detective working tirelessly to pursue a desperate criminal and bring them to justice. Through his career, Pinkerton went after bank robbers and railroad theves, both relatively unknown and infamous like Frank and Jesse James. During the Civil War, he was instrumental in preventing the assassination of Abraham Lincoln and ran an extensive intelligence operation against the South. As America industrialized, his detectives were brought into labor disputes by management seeking to break attempts at unions. This last put a stain on Pinkerton's legacy, a legacy he tried to establish by publishing numerous books about his exploits and the exploits of his detectives. A self-promoter as much as a detective, Allan Pinkerton and his story is a quintessentially American one.

The Pinkerton Agency: The History of Allan Pinkerton and America's First Major Private Detective Organization looks at the life story of the man who formed the detective agency, and the important milestones in the organization's history. Along with pictures depicting important people, places, and events, you will learn about the Pinkertons like never before.

The Pinkerton Agency: The History of Allan Pinkerton and America's First Major Private Detective Organization

A New Start and an Old Calling

As did many men who made their mark on 19th century America, Allan Pinkerton did not start out in the country. In fact, he was born in Glasgow, Scotland, on August 25, 1819, the youngest of three children of William and Isobel Pinkerton. Allan's father was a police sergeant, which no doubt influenced Allan's later career path, but while an important job, it was not a lucrative career. As fate would have it, William died in the line of duty when Allen was 10, leaving the young boy and his family impoverished and forcing him to leave school. He was never to receive another day of formal education, but he remained a voracious reader and became very well educated through his own efforts. In order to support his family, he found work as a cooper (barrel maker).

Sometime after beginning work, Pinkerton became involved with a group called the Chartists, a national movement that advocated for the enactment of the People's Charter, listing reforms designed to give working men representation in Parliament and the right to vote. It was a political rather than an economic or social reform movement, but it attracted workingmen such as Pinkerton who were living in impoverished circumstances. While not much is known about his activities, apparently he was of sufficient notoriety that a warrant was issued by British authorities for his arrest. This prompted him to flee to the United States in 1842, but not before marrying Joan Carfrae on March 13, 1842. With the British authorities nipping at his heels, Pinkerton and his young wife set sail for a new life in America settling in Chicago on their arrival.

The next year, in 1843, the Pinkerton couple moved to Dundee, Illinois, located some 50 miles northwest of Chicago on the Fox River. There Allan built a cabin for himself and his wife and began a cooperage. They were soon joined there by their first child, a daughter named Isabell, in August 1843.

Not content to live a quiet frontier life of a barrel maker, Allan soon began to act on the same reformist impulses that let him to support the Chartists. He became an ardent abolitionist, working for many of the leaders of the abolition movement in Chicago. There is also circumstantial evidence that the Pinkerton's Dundee house served as a stop on the Underground Railroad, the system set up by abolitionists to help escaped slaves flee the Southern states for eventual freedom in Canada. Most of the evidence pointing to Allan's participation in the Underground Railroad comes from the accounts of others, and in the many books he later produced (or had ghostwritten) about his exploits as a detective, he never mentioned participating in it, though he did refer to his ardent support of abolitionism.

Nonetheless, one account documented his supposed assistance to a group led by the fiery abolitionist John Brown: "The most famous slave escape was a group of 12 Freedom Seekers escorted by abolitionist John Brown, John Henry Kagi and Aaron Stevens. In 1857, former Indiana Congressman, Jim Lane had blazed a trail across southern Iowa to Nebraska City, Nebraska turning south and ending at Topeka, Kansas. This trail became known as the Lane

Road. In 1857, the Lane Road became the spine of the Underground Railroad from the Missouri/Kansas border. In the winter of 1858, John Brown's party of Freedom Seekers followed this route north and east through Iowa into Illinois to the Chicago area. At West Liberty, Iowa, William Penn Clarke and J.B. Grinnell arranged for Brown's party to ride in a real railroad train into Chicago. At Chicago, Allan Pinkerton arranged for the party to take a train around Lake Michigan to Detroit. From Detroit, they crossed the Canadian border. The Freedom Seekers were left with Canadian abolitionists."

One of the Freedom Seekers, Sam Harper, gave his firsthand account of this trip in an 1895 interview, but he made no mention of Pinkerton. Regardless, there is little reason to doubt the ardency of Pinkerton's support for abolition, which no doubt motivated his later activities on the side of the Union during the Civil War.

Though it may have seemed inevitable, when Pinkerton eventually found himself following in his father's footsteps, he almost did so by accident. As he would later recount in "How I Became a Detective," the first chapter of his book, *Criminal Reminiscences and Detective Sketches* (as well as several other books he later wrote concerning his career), he was in the woods near Dundee looking for trees appropriate for barrel staves. By his own account, "[O}ne day while busy there I had stumbled upon some smoldering embers and other traces indicating that the little island had been made quite common use of. There was no picnicking in those days—people had more serious matters to attend to—and it required no great keenness to conclude that no honest men were in the habit of occupying the place. As the country was then infested with coin-counterfeiters and desperate horse thieves, from the information I gave, the sheriff of that county (Kane) was able to trace the outlaws to this island, where subsequently I led the officers who captured the entire gang, consisting of men and women, securing their implements and a large amount of bogus coin."

This initial foray into detective work gave Pinkerton somewhat of a reputation in the area as someone who could be relied upon to investigate possible criminal activity. One day, in July 1847, while Allan was at work at his cooperage, he was summoned to the general store of H.E. Hunt. There, the two were joined by another Dundee storekeeper, I.C. Bosworth, and the men asked Pinkerton to help them locate a counterfeiter they believed to be active in the town passing fake $10 bills. Since there was no national currency at the time, frontier towns were dependent on banknotes issued by state-chartered banks for currency, but unfortunately, these notes were easy targets for counterfeiters. In particular, they said a man had recently come into town looking for "Old Man Crane", a man of bad reputation known in the past for working for counterfeiters: "[T]he fact that a respectable appearing man, a stranger well mounted and altogether mysterious, and also well supplied with money, had suddenly shown himself in the village, to begin quietly but searchingly making inquiries for "Old man Crane," seemed to the minds of my friends to be the best of evidence that the stranger was none other than the veritable counterfeiter who was supplying such old reprobates as Crane with the spurious ten-dollar bills"

After protesting that he was hardly the best man for the job, his friends implored him to "do the best you can!" "I suddenly resolved," Pinkerton later recounted, "to do just that and no less; although I must confess that, at that time, I had not the remotest idea how to set about the matter."

The supposed counterfeiter had stopped by the saddlery shop to have repairs made to his saddle, so Pinkerton went to the shop, where he located the suspected counterfeiter. Through providing him some information on how to get to "Old Man Crane," Pinkerton was able to learn that his name was John Craig, gain the man's confidence, and agree to meet him later. Conferring with Hunt and Bosworth, they all agreed Pinkerton should obtain some of the man's stock of counterfeit bills, thus getting the evidence needed to have him arrested. The two shopkeepers gave Allan $50 towards that end, and Pinkerton then rode to meet the Craig. After some time talking, Pinkerton was able to get Craig, who said he was from Vermont, to admit to having sold counterfeit bills to men in other towns. He was also able to gain Craig's confidence, convincing him that he had dealt in counterfeit bills before. Eventually, the man showed him two counterfeit $10 bills, bills that, Pinkerton said, "in all my subsequent detective experience I have hardly seen their equal in point of execution and general appearance."

Having the counterfeiter on the hook, Pinkerton then proceeded to spring the trap. He agreed to purchase some bills, arranging to meet at the site of the unfinished Baptist Church in town. In the process, Craig gave Pinkerton details of his entire operation. Riding back to town, Pinkerton consulted with Hunt and Bosworth, obtained the money he needed to purchase the counterfeit bills, and rode to the Baptist church to meet the counterfeiter. After some anxious moments - he was afraid that he had spooked the criminal when the counterfeiter did not show up at the appointed time - the man appeared ready to do business. He gave Pinkerton 50 counterfeit $10 notes, an amount Pinkerton freely admitted tempted him, but in the end, the would be detective to attempt to capture the counterfeiter and his whole operation through an elaborate ruse that ended a few days later in Chicago, where he went to the local police and told them what he had been up to. Pinkerton said, "After all these arrangements were perfected, I went to the Sauganash Hotel. The officers were merely constables, and one was stationed outside the house, to follow Craig wherever he might go, or whoever might come in contact with him, should he be observed to meet any person with whom he might appear to have confidential relations; while the other officer was located inside the hotel, to cause Craig's arrest whenever the proper time arrived."

Craig showed up at the appointed time, but unfortunately for Pinkerton, Craig got spooked, and went to far as to claim never to have met Pinkerton. Craig was arrested anyway, but he managed to escape justice due to not having any money on his person. Moreover, it turned out he was close friends with the Kane County sheriff into whose custody he had been remanded, and that helped him manage to escape.

Although it was an unfortunate outcome, the entire compelled Pinkerton to take up a career decidedly different from that of cooper.

Forming the Agency and the Start of the Civil War

Due to the notoriety he received from this and other examples of his detective skills, Pinkerton was named a deputy sheriff in Kane County, and in 1849, he was appointed the first police detective in Chicago. He was also employed at certain points by the Post Office Department to investigate incidents of thefts from the mail.

However, he was not content to work for others, and in the spirit of American capitalism, Pinkerton decided to strike out on his own. In 1850, partnering with Edward Rucker, who was a prominent Chicago Attorney, Pinkerton formed the North-Western Police Agency. This was soon renamed the Pinkerton National Detective Agency.

The original company logo

Some of Pinkerton's first cases involved the newest crime: railroad thefts. As the railroad industry grew, so did crimes directed at the trains. By 1855, Pinkerton had a contractual arrangement with the major railroads in the region, including the Illinois Central Railroad. The contract stipulated, "Witnessith; whereas, the said Pinkerton and Company propose to establish a Police Agency, the office of which is to be at Chicago , but which is to operate in the neighbouring states; and whereas it is to be primarily and principally devoted to the service and business of the above named companies, (even to the exclusion of all other business if necessary to the prompt and efficient performance of their business); and whereas, in consideration thereof the said companies have severally agreed to guarantee and pay to said Pinkerton & Co, the several teams hereinafter specified for the first year, to aid them in organizing and putting in effective operation the said agency[.]"

Pinkerton's involvement with the railroads put him in contact with two men who would be very important in his future. The Chief Engineer and Vice President of the Illinois Central Railroad at the time was George McClellan, and its attorney was Abraham Lincoln. He developed a close friendship with McClellan, and McClellan came to trust Pinkerton's skills as a detective. Performing his jobs commendably, McClellan extended the Illinois Central Railroad toward New Orleans and helped the Ohio and Mississippi recover from the Panic of 1857, a financial panic caused by the declining international economy and overexpansion of the domestic economy. During this time, he also used his clout to secure a job as treasurer for his old West Point and Mexico campaign comrade, Ambrose Burnside. All of this would have a monumental impact on the history of the Civil War.

McClellan

Even though he was busy overseeing his burgeoning detective agency and working his own cases, Pinkerton was still active in the abolition movement. By 1859, the divisions in the country over slavery had become deep, and some became convinced that the only way to end slavery was though fomenting a slave rebellion in the Southern states. Pinkerton became involved in a group in Chicago connected to John Brown, attending secret meetings with him and Frederick Douglass, as well as fellow abolitionists John Jones and Henry O. Wagoner. At those meetings, Pinkerton, Jones and Wagoner helped purchase clothes and supplies for Brown, all of which would help lead Brown and his group to attempt to raid the United States arsenal at Harpers Ferry in November 1859 to get the necessary arms and ammunition to arm the freed slaves Brown hoped to attract. The raid failed, and Brown was captured, tried, and hanged.

The fallout from John Brown's raid on Harpers Ferry was intense. Southerners had long suspected that abolitionists hoped to arm the slaves and use violence to abolish slavery, and Brown's raid seemed to confirm that. Meanwhile, much of the northern press praised Brown for his actions. In the South, conspiracy theories ran wild about who had supported the raid, and many believed prominent abolitionist Republicans had been behind the raid as well. On the day of his execution, Brown wrote, "I, John Brown, am now quite *certain* that the crimes of this *guilty land* will never be purged away but with *blood.* I had, as I now think vainly, flattered myself that without very much bloodshed it might be done." John Jones' wife, Mary, believed that the suit Brown wore at his execution was among the supplies Pinkerton and his fellow abolitionists helped purchase.

Pinkerton's commitment to abolitionism and his professional expertise merged with the election of Abraham Lincoln in 1860. Throughout the fall and winter of 1860, Southern calls for secession became increasingly serious. In a last-ditched effort to save the Union, Kentucky's Senator John Crittenden tried to assume the stateliness of his predecessor Henry Clay. Crittenden, however, proved to be no Henry Clay: his proposal that a Constitutional Amendment reinstate the Missouri Compromise line and extend it to the Pacific failed. President Buchanan supported the measure, but President-Elect Lincoln said he refused to allow the further expansion of slavery under any conditions. The Crittenden Compromise failed on December 18. Two days later, South Carolina seceded from the Union. President Buchanan sat on his hands, believing the Southern states had no right to secede, but that the Federal government had no effective power to prevent secession. In January, Mississippi, Florida, Alabama, Georgia, Louisiana and Kansas followed South Carolina's lead. The Confederacy was formed on February 4th, in Montgomery, Alabama, with former Secretary of War Jefferson Davis as its President. On February 23rd, Texas joined the Confederacy.

Lincoln's predecessor was among those who could see the potential conflict coming from a mile away. As the Confederacy continued to grow during his last months in office, President James Buchanan instructed the federal army to permit the Confederacy to take control of forts in its territory, hoping to avoid a war. Conveniently, this also allowed Southern forces to take control of important forts and land ahead of a potential war, which would make secession and/or a victory in a military conflict easier. Many Southern partisans within the federal government at the end of 1860 took advantage of these opportunities to help Southern states ahead of time. One of the forts in the South was Fort Sumter, an important but undermanned and undersupplied fort in the harbor of Charleston, South Carolina. Buchanan attempted to resupply Fort Sumter in the first few months of 1860, but the attempt failed when Southern sympathizers in the harbor fired on the resupply ship.

Rumors flew of plots by pro-slavery forces to assassinate the newly-elected President Lincoln at some point on his journey by train from Illinois to Washington, D.C. for his inauguration. So seriously were these threats taken that the rail company transporting Lincoln and his party contacted Pinkerton's agency to investigate the threats. As Pinkerton later recalled, "I received a letter from Mr. Samuel H. Felton, the president of 'The Philadelphia, Wilmington and Baltimore Railroad,' requesting my presence in Philadelphia upon a matter of great importance… This letter at once aroused me to a realization of the danger that threatened the country, and I determined to render whatever assistance was in my power towards preventing the successful operation of these ill-advised and dangerous men. I lost no time, therefore, in making my arrangements, and soon after receiving Mr. Felton's communication, in company with four members of my force was upon the train speeding towards Philadelphia."

Of all the stops on the route, the one that caused the most concern was Baltimore. Maryland was a slave state and Baltimore was a hotbed of secessionist fervor. Pinkerton later wrote in his book, *Spy of the Rebellion*, "The city of Baltimore was, at this time, a slaveholding city, and the spirit of Slavery was nowhere else more rampant and ferocious…. the mob element of the city of Baltimore—reckless and unscrupulous, as mobs generally are—and this portion of her community were avowedly in full accord with the prospective movement, and ready to do the bidding of the slave power." At their meeting Felton provided Pinkerton with all the information he had about the secessionist threat in Maryland. In order to determine where best to place his men, Pinkerton "took passage on one of the trains of the road, intending to see for myself how affairs stood, and to distribute my men in such a manner as to me seemed best."

Eventually, Pinkerton set up headquarters in Baltimore, which seemed to him to be the center of any possible conspiracy. Pro-secession, anti-Lincoln sentiment so permeated the city that even the local police was dominated by men who held such views, including the chief. Thus, Pinkerton determined to handle the necessary security arrangements, believing that the local forces could not be trusted. He and his agents continued to attempt to ferret out the details of any conspiracy, and he advised the railroad to deploy men to guard the bridges and ferries around the city.

Lincoln left Springfield, Illinois, on February 11, 1861 to begin his journey to the capital for his inauguration. The day before, Pinkerton received a letter claiming that the son of a prominent Maryland citizen had stated that he and several others had taken an oath to assassinate the Lincoln. Pinkerton later wrote, "I determined, therefore, to probe the matter to the bottom, and obtaining the authority of Mr. Felton for such action, I immediately set about the discovery of the existence of the conspiracy and the intention of its organization." He concocted a plan where he and several of his men would be identified as being from New Orleans and Charleston, thus giving people the assumption they were secessionists and thereby gain the trust of those who might be part of a conspiracy. "In looking over the qualifications of the members of my corps," he wrote, "I found two men admirably adapted to the object I had in view. They were both young and both fully able to assume and successfully carry out the character of a hot-blooded, fiery secessionist."

These two, Joseph Howard and Timothy Webster, were able to ingratiate themselves into groups of secessionists. Pinkerton explained, "It was not long before I received undoubted evidence of the existence of a systematized organization whose avowed object was to assist the rebellious States, but which was in reality formed to compass the death of the President, and thus accomplish the separation of the States."

Pinkerton's able men Howard and Webster were able to completely penetrate the group of conspirators, which he claimed included many prominent men of the city, including the City Marshal. Through skillful handling and questioning of one of the members of the conspiracy, Howard was able to get the details of the assassination plot. Lincoln was to be attacked when he arrived in Baltimore on February 23. According to the plotters, while traveling from one depot to another for the final leg of his journey to Washington, a disturbance would draw away his police protection (who would be in on the plot), allowing an assassin to attack him and melt away into the crowd. To prevent the news from getting to the North quickly, telegraph lines from Baltimore were to be cut and bridges leading to the North were to be destroyed.

One of Pinkerton's most resourceful agents was Kate Warne, one of several women the forward-thinking detective employed. He brought her to Baltimore, and once there she made "remarkable progress in cultivating the acquaintance of the wives and daughters of the conspirators." Pinkerton noted, "Mrs. Warne was eminently fitted for this task. Of rather a commanding person, with clear-cut, expressive features, and with an ease of manner that was quite captivating at times, she was calculated to make a favorable impression at once. She was of Northern birth, but in order to vouch for her Southern opinions, she represented herself as from Montgomery, Alabama, a locality with which she was perfectly familiar, from her connection with the detection of the robbery of the Adams Express Company, at that place. Her experience in that case…fully qualified her for the task of representing herself as a resident of the South."

Warne

Pinkerton in the early 1860s

Such was Pinkerton's trust in Warne's skills that he took her with him to New York City to notify Lincoln's party of the details of the conspiracy in Baltimore. Leaving her there to deliver the information, Pinkerton went ahead to Philadelphia. There, after notifying Mr. Felton of the details, a meeting between Pinkerton and Norman Judd, a Representative from Illinois who was accompanying Lincoln on his trip, was arranged. This took place on February 21. At the meeting, Pinkerton laid out all the evidence of the conspiracy. Judd was convinced, and he agreed that security measures needed to be taken. Pinkerton described the meeting in his work: "' My advice is,' said I, after I had succeeded in convincing Mr. Judd that my information was reliable, "that Mr. Lincoln shall proceed to Washington this evening by the eleven o'clock train, and then once safe at the capital, General Scott and his soldiery will afford him ample protection.' ' I fear very much that Mr. Lincoln will not accede to this,' replied Mr. Judd ; 'but as the President is an old acquaintance and friend of yours and has had occasion before this to test your reliability and prudence, suppose you accompany me to the Continental Hotel, and we can then lay this information before him in person and abide by his decision.'"

Lincoln

Judd

Pinkerton went ahead, and though Lincoln was slow to acknowledge the seriousness of the threat, he eventually acceded to the weight of the evidence. Still, he refused to leave Philadelphia that night because he had agreed to raise the flag over Independence Hall and speak before the Pennsylvania legislature at Harrisburg the next day. Beyond that, he would agree to any plan they came up with that would allow him to fulfill these obligations. At a midnight meeting, Pinkerton spelled out the details of his plan: "After the formal reception at Harrisburg had taken place, a special train, consisting of a baggage-car and one passenger-coach, should leave there at six o'clock p. m. to carry Mr. Lincoln and one companion back to Philadelphia…In order to avoid the possibility of accident, the track was to be cleared of everything between Harrisburg and Philadelphia from half-past five o'clock until after the passage of the special train. Mr. Felton was to detain the eleven o'clock p. m. Baltimore train until the arrival of the special train from Harrisburg, Mrs. Warne in the meantime engaging berths in the sleeping-car bound for Baltimore. I was to remain in Philadelphia in order that no accident might occur in conveying the President from one depot to another."

So that word of the change of plans not reach Baltimore, which might allow the conspirators to change their plans to attack Lincoln at some other point on his adjusted route, Pinkerton arranged to have the telegraph line between Harrisburg and Baltimore disrupted.

Lincoln proceeded to fulfill his obligations at Philadelphia and Harrisburg. All went according to plan, and shortly after 10:00 p.m. evening, Lincoln was on a train disguised as Kate Warne's invalid brother. "So carefully had all our movements been conducted," Pinkerton later wrote, "that no one in Philadelphia saw Mr. Lincoln enter the car, and no one on the train, except his own immediate party—not even the conductor, knew of his presence."

The train arrived in Baltimore at 3:00 a.m., and the sleeping car was pulled through the quiet streets to the Washington depot, with no one in the city aware who was inside. After waiting about two hours at the depot for the Washington bound train, Lincoln left Baltimore, arriving in Washington at 6:00 a.m. Pinkerton recalled, "Mr. Lincoln wrapped his traveling shawl about his shoulders, and in company with Mr. Lamon, started to leave the car. I followed close behind, and on the platform found two of my men awaiting our arrival. A great many people were gathered about the depot, but Mr. Lincoln entirely escaped recognition, until as we were about leaving the depot, Mr. Washburne, of Illinois, came up and cordially shook him by the hand. The surprise of this gentleman was unbounded, and many of those standing around, observing his movements, and the tall form of Mr. Lincoln exciting curiosity, I feared that danger might result in case he was recognized at this time. I accordingly went up to them hurriedly, and pressing between them whispered rather loudly: ' No talking here!' Mr. Washburne gazed inquiringly at me, and was about to resent my interference, when Mr. Lincoln interposed: 'That is Mr. Pinkerton, and everything is all right.'"

When the press got wind of the way Lincoln was hidden and rushed to Baltimore, several accounts were sensationalized, giving Lincoln a political black eye before he had even taken office. Of course, this would prove to be a minor problem amid the troubles that lay ahead.

Contemporary cartoons mocking Lincoln about Baltimore

Thanks to the efforts of Pinkerton and his able agents, everything was all right, at least for now. It was unfortunate for President Lincoln, and the nation, that Pinkerton was not in charge of his security that fateful night at Ford's Theatre over four years later.

Pinkerton and McClellan

In his Inauguration Speech, President Lincoln struck a moderate tone. Unlike most Inauguration Addresses, which are typically followed by balls and a "honeymoon" period, Lincoln's came amid a major political crisis. To reassure the South, he reiterated his belief in the legal status of slavery in the South, but that its expansion into the Western territories was to be restricted. He outlined the illegality of secession and refused to acknowledge the South's secession, and promised to continue to deliver U.S. mail in the seceded states. Most importantly, he pledged to not use force unless his obligation to protect Federal property was restricted: "In doing this there needs to be no bloodshed or violence, and there shall be none unless it be forced upon the national authority. The power confided to me will be used to hold, occupy, and posess the property and places belonging to the Government and to collect the duties and imposts; but beyond what may be necessary for these objects, there will be no invasion, no using of force against or among the people anywhere."[1]

Lincoln had promised that it would not be the North that started a potential war, but he was also aware of the possibility of the South initiating conflict. After he was sworn in, Lincoln sent word to the Governor of South Carolina that he was sending ships to resupply Fort Sumter, to which the governor replied demanding that federal forces evacuate it.

Although he vowed not to fire the first shot, Lincoln was likely aware that his attempt to resupply Fort Sumter in Charleston Harbor would draw Southern fire; it had already happened under Buchanan's watch. After his inauguration, President Lincoln informed South Carolina governor Francis Pickens that he was sending supplies to the undermanned garrison at Fort Sumter. When Lincoln made clear that he would attempt to resupply the fort, Davis ordered Beauregard to demand its surrender and prevent the resupplying of the garrison.

In early April, the ship Lincoln sent to resupply the fort was fired upon and turned around. On April 9, Confederate President Davis sent word to General Beauregard to demand the fort's evacuation. At the time, the federal garrison consisted of Major Robert Anderson, Beauregard's artillery instructor from West Point, and 76 troops. Even before the bombardment, upon learning that he was opposed by Beauregard, Anderson remarked that the Southern forces in Charleston harbor would be exercised with "skill and sound judgment". Beauregard also remembered his former superior, and before the bombardment, he sent brandy, whiskey and cigars to Anderson and his garrison, gifts the Major refused.

At 4:30 a.m. on the morning of April 12, 1861, Beauregard ordered the first shots to be fired at

---

1   "Abraham Lincoln, First Inaugural Address." *Presidents: Every Question Answered.* Page 322.

Fort Sumter, effectively igniting the Civil War. After nearly 34 hours and thousands of rounds fired from 47 artillery guns and mortars ringing the harbor, on April 14, 1861, Major Anderson surrendered Fort Sumter, marking the first Confederate victory. No casualties were suffered on either side during the dueling bombardments across Charleston harbor, but, ironically, two Union soldiers were killed by an accidental explosion during the surrender ceremonies.

After the attack on Fort Sumter, support for both the northern and southern cause rose. Two days later, Lincoln issued a call-to-arms asking for 75,000 volunteers. That led to the secession of Virginia, Tennessee, North Carolina, and Arkansas, with the loyalty of border states like Kentucky, Maryland, and Missouri still somewhat up in the air. The large number of southern sympathizers in these states buoyed the Confederates' hopes that those too would soon join the South. Moreover, the loss of these border states, especially Virginia, all deeply depressed Lincoln. Just weeks before, prominent Virginians had reassured Lincoln that the state's historic place in American history made its citizens eager to save the Union. But as soon as Lincoln made any assertive moves to save the Union, Virginia seceded. This greatly concerned Lincoln, who worried Virginia's secession made it more likely other border states and/or Maryland would secede as well.

Still, despite the loss of Fort Sumter and the loss of Virginia, the North expected a relatively quick victory, and their expectations weren't unrealistic, given the Union's overwhelming economic advantages over the South. At the start of the war, the Union had a population of over 22 million. The South had a population of 9 million, nearly 4 million of whom were slaves. Union states contained 90% of the manufacturing capacity of the country and 97% of the weapon manufacturing capacity. Union states also possessed over 70% of the total railroads in the pre-war United States at the start of the war, and the Union also controlled 80% of the shipbuilding capacity of the pre-war United States.

Nine days after war broke out between the Union and the Confederacy after the firing on Fort Sumter, Pinkerton wrote to President Lincoln offering his services "obtaining information on the movements of the traitors, or safely conveying your letters or dispatches." Before receiving an answer, Pinkerton received a summons from his friend and former client, General George McClellan, who asked him to set up a military intelligence operation under his command, the Army Division of the Ohio. Pinkerton readily agreed. Utilizing the same techniques, he had used to such good effect in tracking down railroad bandits and would be assassins, Pinkerton sent agents disguised as Confederate soldiers and sympathizers throughout the South to gather information. It would turn out to be a controversial partnership.

Not content to be merely an administrator, Pinkerton himself went on at least one spy mission himself through the South. Under the guise of a confederate soldier, Major E.J. Allen, he worked across the Deep South in the summer of 1861, recording information on Confederate fortifications and plans. Pinkerton wrote, "I was summoned for consultation with General McClellan....He was desirous of ascertaining, as definitely as possible, the general feeling of the people residing South of the Ohio river, in Kentucky, Tennessee, Mississippi and Louisiana, and requested that measures be at once taken to carry out his purposes. It was essentially necessary at the outset to become acquainted with all the facts that might be of importance hereafter, and no time offered such opportunities for investigations of this nature as the present, while the war movement was in its incipiency, and before the lines between the opposing forces had been so closely drawn as to render traveling in the disaffected district unsafe, if not utterly impossible. As this mission was of a character that required coolness and tact, as well as courage, and as most of my men had been detailed for duties in other sections of the rebellious country, I concluded to make the journey myself, and at once stated my intention to the General, who received it with every evidence of satisfaction and approval."

Beginning in Louisville, he traveled through Kentucky and Tennessee as Major Allen, gathering information about public attitudes and some of the Confederate plans. He arrived at Memphis without incident and was familiar with the city, having visited it a few years before on business for his agency. Now, it was a fully armed Confederate city, and he was truly behind enemy lines. As he later put it, "Here to be known or suspected as a Union man was to merit certain death, and to advocate any theory of compromise between the two sections was to be exiled from the city." He was able to mingle freely with both soldier and civilian, even at one point sitting down to drinks with General Gideon Pillow, who provided Pinkerton with valuable information.

Some of his best sources of information were the slaves employed building fortifications around the city. "From all these sources," Pinkerton later recounted, "I was successful in posting myself fully in regard to the movements and intentions of the rebel authorities and officers, and, as I believed, had also succeeded in concealing my identity."

Unfortunately, Pinkerton was wrong, because he had actually been recognized for who he was after only three days in Memphis. Pinkerton learned of this from a black porter at the hotel he was staying in - one of General Pillow's spies remembered him as someone he had seen in Cincinnati a couple of weeks before. The porter had overheard him and reported the information to Pinkerton. He explained, "This was too important to be ignored. I had no desire to be captured at that time, and I had no doubt of the correctness of the porter's story. I re solved to act at once upon the suggestion, and to make good my escape before it was too late. My admonitory friend was fearfully in earnest about getting me away, and he quickly volunteered to procure my horse, which I had quartered in close proximity to the hotel, and to furnish me with a guide who would see me safely through the lines and outside of the city."

Gathering his belongings, Pinkerton left the hotel through a rear exit and was soon riding out of the city to safety. It was only later, after another of his agents went to Memphis, that he learned the full details of the efforts that were taken to locate and apprehend him.

Having escaped detection in Memphis, Pinkerton decided to continue his mission, so instead of going north to the Union lines, he went further behind enemy lines into Mississippi. He stopped in Jackson, determined to spend a few days scouting the surrounding roads and fortifications. He also made the decision to find a barber to shave his unkempt beard. "This was an unfortunate idea," he recalled, "and I soon had occasion to regret having entertained it for a moment."

Through what could only be described as the wildest of coincidences, the barber recognized him as having been a customer of his in Chicago. Keeping his head, Pinkerton violently denied the barber's allegation, shifting the crowd of curious onlookers to his side through the purchase of several rounds of drinks. That evening, he rode out of town, but not before having purchased his own shaving kit. A few miles outside of Jackson he sold his horse and, convinced he had gathered sufficient intelligence information, returned by a very circuitous route to Cincinnati to report to McClellan.

At this time, McClellan was widely regarded as the Union's finest commander. McClellan will always be associated with losing to Robert E. Lee, but it is often forgotten that McClellan nearly ended Lee's military career in 1861. On May 26, McClellan received intelligence that the critical Baltimore and Ohio Railroad bridges in western Virginia were being burned. As he quickly implemented plans to invade and secure for the Union the region's transportation system, he triggered the first of several political controversies by proclaiming to the citizens of western Virginia that his forces had no intentions of interfering with personal property, including slaves. McClellan's proclamation stated, "Notwithstanding all that has been said by the traitors to induce you to believe that our advent among you will be signalized by interference with your slaves, understand one thing clearly—not only will we abstain from all such interference, but we will on the contrary with an iron hand, crush any attempted insurrection on their part."[2] Immediately realizing that he had overstepped the bounds of his authority, he quickly issued an apologetic letter to President Lincoln for the misstep, but it would be just the first of many public controversies McClellan would instigate by word or action.

Quickly moving his forces through the Virginia area, McClellan achieved several minor military victories, including at the Battle of Philippi Races (June 3, 1861) and at the Battle of Rich Mountain (July 11). Even then, critics of McClellan have accused him of having "an unwarranted sense of caution and reluctance to commit his forces", the descriptions that are still used the most to define his military career. His subordinate commander, General William S. Rosecrans, bitterly complained that McClellan had not reinforced one of their coordinated attacks as agreed. Nevertheless, these two minor victories propelled McClellan to the status of national hero, with The *New York Herald* publishing an article about him entitled, "Gen. McClellan, the Napoleon of the Present War." McClellan himself began circulating flamboyant descriptions of his victories, many of which were reprinted in Northern newspapers.

By July 13, 1861, the Confederate forces in western Virginia had been eliminated, giving the Union control of the land and railroads. West Virginia would become a separate state on June 20, 1863, while the eastern portion maintained the name "Virginia."

---

[2]   Sears, Stephen W. *George B. McClellan: The Young Napoleon.* Pages 79--80.

McClellan's opponent in western Virginia had been General Lee, who was blamed throughout the South for losing western Virginia after his defeat at the Battle of Cheat Mountain. Lee would eventually be reassigned to constructing coastal defenses on the East Coast, and when his men dug trenches in preparation for the defense of Richmond, he was derisively dubbed the "King of Spades". That Lee was even in position to assume command of the Army of Northern Virginia the following year during the Peninsula Campaign was due more to his friendship with Jefferson Davis than anything else. The fact Davis played favorites with his generals crippled the South throughout the war, but it certainly worked in the South's favor with Lee.

On July 22, 1861, the day after Union forces suffered their devastating defeat at Bull Run, President Lincoln summoned McClellan to Washington, providing a special train to bring him from Wheeling through Pittsburgh, Philadelphia, Baltimore, and on to Washington, McClellan was met by enthusiastic crowds and adoring fans at each stop.

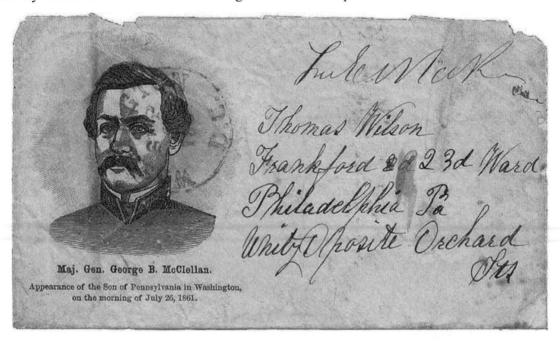

A patriotic cover honoring the arrival of McClellan in Washington, D.C. on July 26, 1861

Upon his arrival on July 26, McClellan was placed in command of the Department of the Potomac (the Union Army of the East), charged with defending the Union capital and the destruction of the Confederate forces in northern and eastern Virginia.

In November of 1861, upon the retirement of General Winfield Scott, the 35 year old McClellan assumed the office of General-in-Chief of the Army of the Potomac, an office he would only hold four months. Common military scuttlebutt of the time said the reason Scott was urged to retire was that he'd gotten too fat to sit a horse -- and could no longer ride into combat. With the deference to McClellan and the defeat at Bull Run, Scott was feeling squeezed out of his role as Congressmen and Lincoln communicated directly with McClellan. The McClellan-Scott relationship has often been portrayed as McClellan intriguing to have Scott removed. By August, McClellan was telling his wife that Scott was a "dotard or traitor" and that Scott was his strongest antagonist. However, it seems likely that Scott was on his way out regardless of any role McClellan could have or could not have played.

Historians who are critical of McClellan's generalship in the field are unanimous in their praise of McClellan's organizational skills. Displaying outstanding organizational and logistical skills, General McClellan quickly whipped the disheartened Union Army into a tight-knit fighting unit with high morale, a highly efficient staff, and optimal supporting services. Just as much, the nearly 175,000 man army loved "Little Mac". McClellan also turned Washington D.C. into the most fortified spot on the continent, ringing it with forts that would make the city all but invulnerable to attack if manned.

All that now lay ahead was for McClellan to take the offensive Lincoln had entrusted in him; to march his men into the Southern states and capture Richmond and demolish Confederate forces in the process. But even by the fall of 1861, Little Mac, as he was now commonly called, still refused to follow President Lincoln's mandate, claiming that his army was still unprepared. Displaying both arrogance and reluctance to fight, McClellan demanded more men, supplies, and time to better prepare, refusing to even meet with the President to share his plan of attack on the Confederate capital. As Lincoln's frustrations began to grow, McClellan's stated opposition to emancipation of slaves angered the Radical Republicans who comprised an important bloc in Congress.

Pinkerton continued to work as McClellan's intelligence officer after the general took command of the Army of the Potomac. In this regard, it is important to remember that there was no Union Army intelligence service as such. Each individual army command had their own spies, and their intelligence operations reported to the generals in charge of the Army. As such, Pinkerton's later claim to have been "Chief of the United States Secret Service" was somewhat of an exaggeration. Given his penchant for self-promotion, however, it is not surprising.

After moving with McClellan to the Army of the Potomac, Pinkerton became directly involved in an operation to apprehend Rose Greenhow. Rose Greenhow was a Confederate spy who used her fashionable home in Washington and her social connections to obtain information on Union activities and pass it on to the Confederate government in Richmond. Pinkerton put her house in Washington under surveillance and gathered around him several men and women to assist him, but Pinkerton could not resist investigating himself. On a rainy night, he went to a high window and, while standing on the shoulders of two of his operatives, peeked in her parlor "prepared to take notes of what transpired." He noticed a Captain assigned to the provost marshal's office show Greenhow a map. After the officer left, Pinkerton followed him to a building he did not recognize. From the building emerged four soldiers with fixed bayonets, who arrested Pinkerton on the Captain's orders. Soon, however, Pinkerton was able to establish his credentials; he was released and the Captain, who later committed suicide, was arrested. A week later, Pinkerton arrested Greenhow at her home and seized documents that detailed her work as well and her romantic connections with two sitting Senators. She was charged with being a spy and in June 1862 sent through the Union and Confederate lines to Richmond.

Pinkerton continued as McClellan's spy chief through the campaign to Richmond, supplying McClellan with estimates of Confederate strength based on information Pinkerton received from his spies behind the lines. Today, McClellan is often derisively mocked for being too cautious, but Pinkerton played a seminal role in the subsequent military decisions he made at the start of 1862. McClellan's Peninsula Campaign has been analyzed meticulously and is considered one of the grandest failures of the Union war effort, with McClellan made the scapegoat. In actuality, there was plenty of blame to go around, including Lincoln and his administration, which was so concerned about Stonewall Jackson's army in the Shenandoah Valley that several Union armies were left in the Valley to defend the capital, and even more were held back from McClellan for fear of the capital's safety. The administration also micromanaged the deployment of certain divisions, and with Secretary of War Stanton's decision to shut down recruiting stations in early 1862, combined with the Confederacy concentrating all their troops in the area, the Army of the Potomac was eventually outnumbered in front of Richmond. At the beginning of the campaign, however, McClellan had vastly superior numbers at his disposal, with only about 70,000 Confederate troops on the entirety of the peninsula and fewer than 17,000 between him and the Capital). McClellan was unaware of this decisive advantage, however, because of the intelligence reports he kept receiving from Pinkerton that vastly overstated the number of available Confederate soldiers. According to Pinkerton, the Confederates outnumbered McClellan's army by nearly double his strength.

The same thing would happen a few months later at Antietam. McClellan's army, which may have outnumbered Lee's forces by about 50,000 men, confronted the Confederates around the night of September 16. By the end of the afternoon, Union attacks on the flanks and the center of the line had been violent but eventually unsuccessful. Fearing that his army was badly bloodied and figuring Lee had many more men than he did, McClellan refused to commit his reserves to continue the attacks, unnerved by Fitz John Porter telling him, "Remember, General, I command the last reserve of the last Army of the Republic." Thus, the day ended in a tactical stalemate.

After the battle, McClellan wrote to his wife, "Those in whose judgment I rely tell me that I fought the battle splendidly and that it was a masterpiece of art. ... I feel I have done all that can be asked in twice saving the country. ... I feel some little pride in having, with a beaten & demoralized army, defeated Lee so utterly. ... Well, one of these days history will I trust do me justice." Historians have generally been far less kind with their praise, criticizing McClellan for not sharing his battle plans with his corps commanders, which prevented them from using initiative outside of their sectors. McClellan also failed to use cavalry in the battle; had cavalry been used for reconnaissance, other fording options might have prevented the debacle at Burnside's Bridge.

Despite heavily outnumbering the Southern army and badly damaging it during the battle of

Antietam, McClellan never did pursue Lee across the Potomac, citing shortages of equipment and the fear of overextending his forces. General-in-Chief Henry W. Halleck wrote in his official report, "The long inactivity of so large an army in the face of a defeated foe, and during the most favorable season for rapid movements and a vigorous campaign, was a matter of great disappointment and regret." Lincoln sardonically referred to the Army of the Potomac as General McClellan's bodyguard, and in one October message to McClellan, Lincoln didn't bother trying to conceal his disgust, writing, "I have just read your dispatch about sore-tongued and fatigued horses, Will you pardon me for asking what the horses of your army have done since the Battle of Antietam that fatigues anything?"

Some of Lincoln's assertions make clear his lack of familiarity with military matters. McClellan still had to deal with the logistical reorganization of his army and the rehabilitation after having suffered about 10,000 casualties in one day. And as Lincoln grew more disenchanted with McClellan, specifically the state of inertia along the Potomac, Jeb Stuart rode around McClellan's army for the second time in early October, displaying just how unable the Union forces were to cover the Potomac crossings.

McClellan also faced growing public pressure and pressure from the administration to advance before the midterm elections. McClellan wished to wait until Spring of 1863 to resume active campaigning, hoping once again to use the Peninsula, but he was compelled to move by mid-October. McClellan saw the campaign as merely a temporary way of placating the administration before positioning his army around Fredericksburg to plan for the following Spring.

Lincoln had finally had enough of McClellan's "slows", and his constant excuses for not taking forward action. Lincoln relieved McClellan of his command of the Army of the Potomac on November 7, 1862, effectively ending the general's military career. Once again using the media to deflect his inadequacies, McClellan blamed Washington for having not sent more men and equipment before mounting the Antietam offensive. Lincoln reportedly responded, "Sending reinforcements to McClellan is like shoveling flies across a barn." McClellan's military career was essentially over, having ended in disgrace.

While McClellan's decision to employ members of what was still essentially a railroad security agency proved a serious misstep in that they were not trained in military operations and therefore woefully inadequate to assess them, McClellan was clearly on the right track. And while Major General Joseph Hooker is credited with founding the Bureau of Military Information in January of 1863, there can be little doubt that it was prompted by what McClellan had initially called his "National Detective Agency."

Pinkerton, Lincoln, and General John McClernand visiting Antietam after the battle

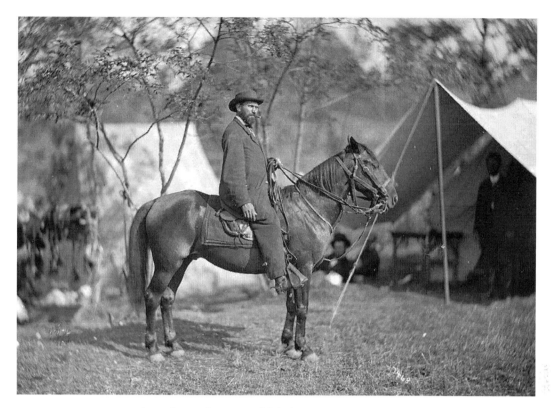

Another picture of Pinkerton at Antietam

Pinkerton resigned his position shortly after McClellan was sacked, but while he would no longer be involved in military intelligence, Pinkerton continued to work for the government. He was employed in investigating the numerous claims filed against the government for losses of property on account of the war. "While acting in this capacity," Pinkerton later wrote, "I was instrumental in unearthing a vast number of fraudulent claims, and, in bringing to justice a large number of men who were engaged in the base attempt to swindle and defraud the nation in the dark hours of her need and peril."

Pinkerton was transferred to New Orleans, by that time under Union occupation, in early 1864, where he primarily examined cotton claims and uncovered the frauds that people sought to perpetrate against the government. His involvement in the war only ended when the conflict did, after which Pinkerton returned to Chicago and resumed the normal operations of his agency.

Outlaws and the Frontier

The end of the war did not provide Pinkerton and his detectives any time to relax. After the war ended, former guerrillas were mostly able to return to their civilian homes and jobs and get on with their lives, but some would continue their bushwhacking ways. These gangs were made up of men who had fought for either the Union or the Confederacy (sometimes both at different times) and had no compunction about committing acts of violence in pursuit of gain. As a result, war veterans like Cole Younger and Jesse James would form posses in the West and become some of the most famous men of their time robbing banks and trains.

Due to the virtually nonexistent nature of law enforcement in frontier areas, Pinkerton's agents were employed by banks and railroad companies to hunt down the gangs and bring them to justice. The first major post-Civil War gang Pinkerton and his agency went after was the Reno Gang. Centered in Jackson County, Indiana, the Reno Gang operated in Indiana and Missouri in the late 1860s, robbing banks and county treasuries. The gang consisted of the Reno brothers (John, Frank, Simeon, and William), along with a cadre of counterfeiters, ruffians, and petty thieves. The Reno brothers started small, playing crooked card games with travelers and engaging in other small cons. During the Civil War, they engaged in "bounty jumping," the practice of joining the army for recruitment money, deserting the post, and pocketing the cash. After returning home, the Reno brothers formed a gang with other bounty jumpers and undertook a series of small robberies in the community.

Frank Reno

John Reno

Their activities took a major leap on October 8, 1866, when John Reno, Simeon Reno, and Frank Sparks robbed the Ohio and Mississippi Railway express car. It is considered one of the first major train robberies in American history, and the gang followed this escapade up over the next couple of years with a series of robberies in the surrounding area, targeting banks, country treasuries, and railroad express companies to the tune of hundreds of thousands of dollars.

Frank Sparks

By 1867, the Reno Gang was so notorious that a bunch of copycats took their cues and started imitating them. In fact, a couple of these copycats spelled the beginning of the end for the Reno Gang. As Justin Clark noted in "Outlaws, Pinkertons, and Vigilantes: the Reno Gang and its Enemies," "On September 28, 1867, copycats Walker Hammond and Michael Colleran robbed the Adams Express on the Ohio and Mississippi railroad, almost a year after the Renos' attempt, and made off with $10,000. Hammond and Colleran, while successful in their robbery, were not successful in their escape. The Renos knew their plans and watched the hold-up from afar, and as the copycats attempted their getaway, the gang cut them off and 'relieved the robbers of their plunder.' In an even brasher move, the Renos left Hammond and Colleran to the authorities, where they served time while the gang got away with their cash. This appeared to be the last straw for the community and for the Adams Express Company. As a response to constant terror, Adams Express employed Allan Pinkerton, the famous private detective, and his agents to hunt down the Renos."

Shortly after the Pinkertons were brought in, John Reno and Frank Sparks carried out a series of robberies in Missouri. Returning to Indiana, Pinkerton and his men surrounded Reno's train and arrested him. Later, Pinkerton arrested Sparks near Seymore. John Reno was sent back to Missouri for trial, where he was convicted of safe robbing and sentenced to 25 years in prison.

In spite of John's imprisonment, the Reno Gang continued under the leadership of Frank Reno into the summer of 1868, and they conducted one of their most successful robberies on May 22 when they robbed the Adams Express on the Jeffersonville line in Marshfield, 17 miles south of Seymour. The robbers pocketed almost $96,000 by cracking three safes, but it proved to be the Reno Gang's last successful train robbery. On July, 10, 1868, the gang tried robbing an express on the Ohio and Mississippi line, but this time, however, they received "a volley from the pistols of the guard inside." The robbers were driven off, and as the *Terre Haute Daily Express* later reported, "A party of men who were hunting the thieves chased the gang into a thicket near Rockford, Indiana." The party of men described in the article were Pinkertons, and furthermore, they succeeded in capturing one member of the gang named Charles Roseberry, whom they brought into nearby Rockford, Indiana, for medical treatment and questioning. The other members of the gang who participated in the robbery attempt - John Moore, Henry Jerrell, and Frank Sparks - escaped with severe injuries.

In rapid succession, the Reno Gang broke up. Frank Reno fled to Canada and started a new life, but other members of the gang were not so fortunate. By the end of 1868, most of the members of the gang had been captured by local "vigilance committees," which often meant the culprits faced summary justice in the form of lynching. The more fortunate ones were captured and brought to justice by the Pinkertons. In August, Frank Reno and his associate Charles Anderson were arrested in Windsor for the Adams Express robbery. They were extradited under the guard of Pinkerton and his men. The two tried to escape, but the Pinkertons were ready for their antics and they successfully delivered Reno and Anderson back to the United States.

Among Pinkerton's most famous investigations involved his work in trying to track down the infamous Jesse James. Jesse, along with his brother Frank, were pro-secessionists in Civil War Missouri who were suspected of participating in several atrocities committed against pro-Union communities. After the war, the brothers used the skills they learned during the war to engage in a life of crime.

Jesse James and Frank James in the 1870s

The James brother's first robbery may have been of the Clay County Savings Association in Liberty, Missouri, on February 13, 1866, but the evidence of their involvement is purely circumstantial. What is not circumstantial is that after this robbery, many others were committed by the James brothers that increased their notoriety, not only in Missouri but throughout the West. The brothers hit the big time with their robbery of the Daviess County Savings Association in Gallatin, Missouri, on December 7, 1869; while the pair netted little money, Jesse shot and killed the cashier after mistaking him for a former pro-Union militia officer. The robbers subsequently boasted that they had killed Major Samuel P. Cox, and while it was a case of mistaken identity, it is significant that they were justifying their robbery by settling an old score.

Naturally, Jesse's boasts about killing Cox had the effect of implicating him in the robbery and murder, and Gallatin was in an uproar. The governor of Missouri offered a reward for the capture of Jesse and Frank, and the *St. Joseph Gazette* provided details of the robbery and murder. Mentioning Jesse and Frank by name as the suspects, the article marked the first time that Jesse's name appeared in print in connection to a crime. It was exactly what Jesse had been waiting for.

For a man who spent much of his brief life seeking attention, he had it now, and with the help of a newspaperman from Kansas City, Jesse James would soon become a household name.

From that point on, the James brothers grew in notoriety. In the early 1870s, the James brothers joined with Cole Younger and his brothers to form the James-Younger gang. There has been much speculation about the inner workings of the James-Younger gang. The group was a fluid one, with members coming and going and different jobs requiring larger or smaller numbers of men. It's also unclear who was in charge. Since these were independent-minded criminals and former guerrillas, much was probably done on consensus, with Frank James and Cole Younger as the leading thinkers. After all, they were older and had the most war experience. Jesse James was certainly the most outspoken member of the group. He was constantly sending letters to the press proclaiming his innocence and stating that he would appear in court if he thought he could get a fair trial, but it appears to have been his older and more level-headed brother Frank, along with Cole Younger, who made most of the decisions. One member of the gang, George Shepard, who was captured shortly after the robbery of the Southern Bank of Kentucky on March 21, 1868, said in a newspaper interview, "Frank is the most shrewd, cunning, and capable; in fact, Jesse can't compare with him. Frank is a man of education, and can act the fine gentleman on all occasions. Jesse is reckless, and a regular dare-devil in courage, but it's Frank makes who all the plans and perfects the methods of escape. Jesse is a fighter and that's all. . .[Frank] would rather not be known, so he directs Jesse and Jesse directs the crowd. He [Jesse] likes notoriety and always takes care to let the people on trains know that he is the leader, and he always enjoyed the reading of his exploits in the papers."

The secretive and mercurial nature of the gang allowed members to claim innocence of individual crimes even when they were implicated as being part of the group. In his autobiography, Cole wrote that "right here I want to state, and I will take my oath solemnly that what I say is the truth, and *nothing but the truth, notwithstanding all the accusations that have been made against me, I never, in all my life, had anything whatever to do with robbing any bank in the state of Missouri.* I could prove that I was not in the towns where banks were robbed in Missouri, at the time that the raids took place, and in many instances that I was thousands of miles away."

John Newman Edwards was a former officer in the Confederate army who worked as an editor at the *Kansas City Times*. An alcoholic who was still bitter over the war, he was eager to stir up the former Confederates within the Democratic Party. His interests were purely political, as he wanted the ex-Confederates to resume their place of power. He saw the story in the *Gazette* about Jesse and Frank James and, with it, an opportunity to spread propaganda about the former Confederates of the Civil War, which in turn could potentially help his cause. He had already shown no hesitancy to portray armed rebels as victims of radicals from the North.

Edwards

Edwards met with Frank and Jesse and quickly realized that Jesse sought the limelight far more than Frank did. Jesse possessed almost an urgency to be noticed and this played well into Edwards' desire to create a story about the unfair treatment of ex-Confederates. About six months after the robbery in Gallatin, Jesse wrote an open letter to the governor, which Edwards printed in the *Times*. Jesse claimed that he was innocent of the charges against him and that the Union men were the true criminals. Jesse said that he was being unfairly cast as an outlaw simply because he held beliefs that were different from the Union. The creation of the mythical Jesse James was underway.

It was Edwards who started the myth that Jesse was the modern-day Robin Hood who stole from the rich to give to the poor. In 1873, he devoted 20 pages to the James gang, glorifying their achievements as noble and for the greater good. Jesse was so enamored with the image that Edwards would create for him that he named his son, Jesse Edward James, after Edwards, although Jesse, Jr. was known as Tim. To make sure there was no doubt that he had been there, Jesse even took to leaving press releases at his crime scenes. He had no difficulty trying to live up to the image Edwards created, usually dressing in style and carrying a Bible that looked like it had been referred to often.

The James and Younger brothers moved freely about their home turf in Missouri, and thanks to Edwards, the public was convinced that the gang was on a noble pursuit. Not only did state residents refuse to turn the gang in, they helped shield them from the law, making the task of finding the gang very difficult for Missouri authorities. This coincided with ex-Confederates winning back their seats in the state Senate. The conditions were ripe for the mythical Jesse to flourish.

In the next few years the gang seemed to be everywhere, hitting banks and stagecoaches in Missouri and Arkansas. Jesse James got into the habit of writing letters to the papers proclaiming his innocence while at the same time saying he was a fugitive because of Yankee persecution. Of course, as the gang's fame spread, so did their supposed robberies; they were only one of many gangs riding the countryside committing robberies, but most crimes were laid at their door.

On June 3, 1871, the gang was certainly involved in a job up in Iowa. Cole Younger, Clell Miller, and Frank and Jesse James robbed the Obocock Brothers bank of Corydon of $6,000. This time the heist was better planned. Most of the town was in the yard of the local Methodist church listening to a politician speak, but while the bandits had gotten away with no gunplay, they couldn't resist a bit of showmanship. One of the robbers rode up and announced to the crowd that the bank had been robbed. Everyone figured he was a heckler and ignored him, only to find out later he had been speaking the truth.

A portrait of Clell Miller

That crime brought additional attention to Jesse James, and it was an indication that James and his gang were operating across multiple states. In fact, the gang would operate as far south as Texas and as far east as West Virginia. Powerless to stop outlaws like James, banks began turning to the Pinkerton Detective Agency in an attempt to track them down.

Allan's son Robert was sent to Missouri to find Jesse and Frank, and with the assistance of a local sheriff, Robert Pinkerton tracked the gang to a farm in rural Missouri. However, the gang got away and a few weeks later, Jesse sent another letter to the local press, again claiming that he was an innocent victim.

In 1872, the gang rolled into Columbia, Kentucky, intent on robbing a bank. When the cashier, R.A.C. Martin refused to open the safe, one of the bandits turned to leave, then turned back around and shot the man in cold blood. Later that year, Jesse and two of the Younger brothers went to the Second Annual Kansas City Industrial Exposition. In front of thousands of witnesses, they robbed a ticket booth and got away with about $900, but a little girl was shot in the fight with the ticket seller. Jesse again wrote a letter to the paper, denying any involvement by him or the Youngers in harming the child. However, Cole Younger was furious that his name was being mentioned in print in any capacity with the crime. Edwards seized the opportunity to write an editorial titled "The Chivalry of Crime" and compared the bandits to President Ulysses S. Grant, the former Union general. Edwards said that Grant had stolen millions of dollars from Americans, whereas Jesse and his gang stole from the rich to give to the poor.

The gang carried out a series of robberies that ranged from West Virginia to Texas and included banks, stagecoaches, and even a fair in Kansas City, but in 1873, they graduated to robbing trains, carrying off the contents of the express safes in baggage cars on numerous trains. This prompted the Adams Express Company, as they had with the Reno Gang, to hire Pinkterton to go after the James-Younger gang and end its criminal activities.

Pinkerton was particularly interested in going after the gang because of their pro-Confederate past. In fact, Jesse James had written letters to the editors of several newspapers in Missouri expressing his continuing sympathy for the Lost Cause as well as criticizing Republican policies towards the former Confederate states. The former Union spy no doubt saw going after Jesse James and his gang as finishing up some leftover business from the Civil War, much the way Jesse James thought he was settling scores.

One of the many challenges faced in tracking down the James gang was the support they received from former Confederate soldiers in Missouri. Pinkerton began his operation by sending one of his agents, a young man named Joseph Whicher, to infiltrate the farm of Zerelda James Samuel, the mother of Frank and Jesse James. Zerelda at the time was living there with her third husband, Dr. Reuben Samuel, and their four children, including their 8-year-old son Archie. Amy Crawford in *Smithsonian* described Zerelda as "mean, ugly and strong-willed, as well as a dedicated slaveholder and secessionist. Still angry about the way the war had turned out, Samuel saw Jesse and Frank, the sons by her first marriage, as freedom fighters for the downtrodden southern states, rather than mere bandits and murderers."

When Whicher got to Clay County and asked where Jesse lived, the sheriff advised him not to go out there. He told Whicher if one of the James boys didn't kill him, their mother would. It's not known what happened, but Whicher was found bound, tortured, and shot in the woods near Zerelda's farm not long after he arrived. Whicher's body had six bullet holes and a note pinned to him saying that such a fate would happen to agents who went looking for the James brothers.

Undeterred, on January 5, 1874, a gang of five men, including Cole, stopped a stagecoach near Hot Springs, Arkansas, and demanded the passengers give up their watches, jewelry, and cash. Cole asked the startled civilians if any of them were Confederate veterans. When one said he had fought for the South, Cole returned his money and watch, declaring that "they didn't want to rob Confederate soldiers; that the Northern men had driven them to outlawry and they intended to make them pay for it." This time, the gang got away with about $2,000 and several watches and pieces of jewelry.

Later that same month, the gang performed one of their most famous heists. On January 31, five members of the gang descended upon the tiny railway town of Gads Hill. This isolated hamlet had a population of only 15 and wouldn't have even existed if it weren't for the railway. The gang wasn't looking to rob the town, though; they were looking to rob the Little Rock Express that was due that afternoon.

The gang quickly rounded up the locals and robbed the settlement's one store of about $750. The townspeople were allowed to build a bonfire to keep out the cold and were instructed not to move. At 5:15, the Little Rock Express approached Gads Hill. One of the robbers waved a red flag from the station platform, an emergency signal to stop. As the train slowed, it moved onto a siding. The bandits had flipped the switch.

The train screeched to a halt and the five bandits converged on the train. Within moments, the crew was under guard and the gang climbed aboard. First they searched the express car. In the days before wire transfers and checking accounts, money had to be shipped in cash, and it was the job of express agents to guard the safes as they sped across the country in express cars. The bandits told Alford to keep quiet if he didn't want to get his head blown off. After robbing the baggage car, they moved on to the safe in the Adams Express car, which netted them over $1,000. Before moving on, they took the conductor's revolver and tobacco. From there, it was on to the passenger car. Alford recalled, "They weren't careful with the passengers. They punched them in the ribs with pistols and pointed their shooting irons into their faces. Not a man escaped. Everyone was robbed…" Those robbed included a sleeping car porter, who forked over his two dollars, and a "train boy" was relieved of $40. As the bandits made their way through the train, Frank quoted Shakespeare, one of the men wrote "robbed at Gads Hill" in a receipt book, and another outlaw exchanged hats with one of the passengers. A travelling reverend was spared this treatment and was asked to pray for the robbers' souls.

All told, the bandits found more than $5,000 in cash and bonds. Deciding to have some fun, one of the bandits asked for the receipt book and wrote in it "Robbed at Gads Hill." Once they had what they came for, the gang told the crew that they could get on their way and handed over a telegram to be sent to the *Saint Louis Dispatch* once they got to their destination. It read:

> "The most daring robbery on record. The southbound train on the Iron Mountain Railroad was robbed here this evening by five heavily armed men, and robbed of . . . dollars. The robbers arrived at the station a few minutes before the arrival of the train, and arrested the Agent, put him under guard, and then threw the train on the switch. The robbers are all large men, none of them under six feet tall. They were all masked, and started in a southerly direction after they had robbed the train, all mounted on fine blooded horses. There is a hell of excitement in this part of the country.
>
> (signed) Ira A. Merrill."

Pinkerton was furious and swore to get the James brothers and their gang. He is reported to have said, "When we meet, it must be the death of one or both of us."

On January 25, 1875, the Pinkertons took another run at the James boys when three of the agents, with backup from Clay County locals, surrounded Zerelda's house. Shortly after midnight, Pinkerton ordered that the James farmhouse be firebombed. At this point, he was embarrassed and desperate, willing to try anything.

An account of the raid was published in the Jefferson City, Missouri *State Journal* on January 29, 1875: "Thursday Morning about half past one o'clock, Mr. Samuels, the stepfather of the James boys, awoke, and found Mrs. Samuels in the same condition. He said he heard a noise in the kitchen, and thought he smelled fire. At this he got out of bed and went out of the door of his room to go into the kitchen. When he got outside he discovered the west end of the kitchen to be on fire.

Samuels went around to where the fire was and set about to try to get the fire out. Zerelda had by that time come from her room with her children. When she got to the kitchen, she found her black servant with her three children up. Zerelda found a quilt on the bed of fire, which the proceeded to tear off and throw out of doors. It was at that point that she spotted something unusual:

> "She then discovered something on the floor which she took to be a turpentine ball. It was on fire. She attempted to pick it up but found it too heavy. She then tried to push it into the fire with her foot, but failed. At this moment Mr. Samuels came in, having extinguished the flames, and he tried to kick the supposed ball into the fire , but failed. He then took a shovel and threw it into the fireplace. As he did this it

exploded. It was a bomb, correctly speaking, what is known as a hand grenade, a ball about one inch in thickness and lined with wrought iron.

The grenade had a devastating effect on all those who were in close proximity to it. A portion struck Dr. Samuels on the right side of the head, but fortunately only wounded him. Zerelda took a piece of the grenade in her arm which shattered a few inches above her right wrist. The worst of the explosion was received by young Archie; a fragment struck him under his third rib on the left hand side, penetrating his bowel. He died from his injuries a couple of hours later. Zerelda, suffering great pain from her injuries, had to have her arm amputate to just below the elbow."

The next morning, the local sheriff came to investigate the scene: "The tracks of horses were discovered leading from the barn to a spot in the horse lot. In the rear of the ice house (east of dwelling) were found the tracks of four or five men. The fence on a diagonal line from the ice house to the horse lot was found to be riddled with balls. In the vicinity of the blood in the horse lot there were indications which showed that the horses have suddenly turned and went off in a northwesterly direction of the barn, then went into a wheat field. Blood was discovered at this spot and all along the route the horses went as far as they could be traced. On the west side of the barn it was found that a horse had been hitched. Mr. Samuels says he heard a horse going at a rapid rate from that point down west of the house, through the "woods" on the south, an around the "ice-house." Three men were tracked in a northeasterly direction for some distance and then west to a spot on the Haynesville road where it was found that seven horses had been tied. A navy, loaded, was found in front of the ice-house."

Having laid out the events, the article began to speculate as to who was responsible for the attack. It was clear that the raid on the James farm aimed to capture of Frank and Jesse James, and there was no doubt in the mind of the reporter that the Pinkertons were involved. The newspaper told readers, "On the night of the battle the Incoming train on the Hannibal and St. Joe. road, bound west, was flagged about a mile and a half west of Kearney, and four men got off the train. This same thing occurred at the same place about a week ago. Again, it Is stated that a locomotive and caboose left this city at midnight, of the same date, and in it were several men known to have been Pinkerton's Chicago detectives; that the lines between here and Cameron were not in operation; that early in the morning this same engine and caboose were seen to pass Chllllcollie, and It was understood that the James boys were in the caboose heavily Ironed. The conclusion would appear to be that the men who got off the train a week ago were detectives who were on the lay; that they ascertained what they wanted, and the caboose of Tuesday night contained others, and that others got off the train when It stopped a mile and a half beyond a station…Just how fur a band of detectives , or anybody else, should go in their attempt to capture outlaws is not definitely known. If they have to resort to throwing bombshells into a family of innocent children and women, it is questionable whether their efforts to rid the country of bandits will accomplish their purposes. Two wrongs never made a right. The hand grenade introduced on this occasion is simply barbarous."

Other newspapers published criticisms of Pinkerton's attack on the James farmstead. The *Nashville Union and American* reported, "The late attack upon their mother's house is a wrong they will never forgive and unless we are greatly mistaken, those who were implicated in that shameful and cowardly assault will yet rue the day that they ever heard the names of Frank and Jesse James. It is now war to the death between the James boys and Pinkerton's assassins."

The general outrage at the reported actions of Pinkerton and his men, not so much in support of the James brothers but that the detectives had acted in an extralegal manner seeking vengeance for the loss agents, prompted the Missouri legislature to pass a resolution: "That the Governor be respectfully requested to inquire into the truth of the said reports, and to employ such agents therefor as he may deem necessary, and report to the General Assembly, at as early a date as practicable, such facts as he may consider compatible with the public interest; and also, if it shall be found that the state of Missouri has been wantonly invaded, as is charged, by an unauthorized force, or that having been possessed of authority such force or posse has transcended the same and disregarded the rights of citizens of this State, that he shall communicate such finding to this Assembly, in order that the dignity and sovereignty of the State may be asserted, its laws vindicated, and such legislation be had, if needed, as will bring the offenders to speedy punishment."

Responding to the stories and the criticism, Pinkerton at first denied that he or his men had anything to do with firebombing the James farmhouse. Later, the detectives claimed that they had thrown a flare into the farmhouse to illuminate the interior, but that Zerelda and her husband had kicked it into the fireplace, with the hot coals causing the explosion. This was the official story for over 100 years, though historians doubted that it was true. When Pinkerton biographer Ted Yeatman was going through the files of the Agency at the Library of Congress, he came across letters concerning the raid on "Castle James," as Pinkerton referred to the farm. Pinkerton's final instructions were pretty clear: "Above everything, destroy the house to the fringe of the ground. . . . Let the men take no risk, burn the house down."

To say that the Pinkerton attack was a disaster would be an understatement, and after that episode public sentiment was now squarely in the bandits' favor. Some in Missouri's state government even went so far as to propose a bill offering the James-Younger gang amnesty, a measure that was barely defeated, and many people came to believe that Jesse was telling the truth and truly was a victim of a manhunt by vicious radicals.

Most also correctly suspected that this obviously illegal act by the Pinkertons would not go unanswered. The underground intelligence system that aided the James brothers told them that Jack Ladd was the Pinkerton detective who threw the grenade and that he had infiltrated the area by working on Daniel Askew's farm. Jesse and Frank pursued Ladd for over a week before discovering that he had left the state, but Askew was easier to find, given that he lived a short distance from their mother's farm. Jesse rode out to Askew's house on April 12, 1875, not knowing for sure what Askew did but not caring for an explanation. Upon confronting Askew,

James shot him to death in his yard. Allen Pinkerton's dream of catching Jesse James was finished.

In addition to that, two Pinkerton detectives and a local deputy sheriff began a sweep in St. Clair County, a known hideout for the Younger brothers. They posed as cattle buyers in order to have an excuse to ride around all the back roads and ask questions of the locals. As chance would have it, the lawmen happened upon a farm where Jim and John Younger were holed up. While the desperados hid in a back room, guns at the ready, the farmer chatted with the "cattle buyers" for a time before sending them on their way.

Of course, Jim and John's suspicions were aroused by this. They were always wary of strangers and the story about the trio being cattle buyers didn't ring true, so the Youngers decided to follow them and see what they were up to. They mounted up, each with their weapons ready. Jim had a revolver and John toted a double-barreled shotgun.

The lawmen hadn't gotten far, and as the Younger brothers drew up behind them they turned into their saddles, alerted by the clopping of hooves on the dirt road. The brothers aimed their weapons and ordered the men to give up their guns. One of the Pinkertons panicked and galloped away, getting his hat shot off in the process. The other two tried to remain calm, keeping their hands in the air and insisting they were nothing but cattle buyers.

The Younger brothers took their weapons and there followed a moment of tense silence. The lawmen understood full well that they were likely to be killed; other officers of the law had lost their lives in the hunt for the James-Younger gang, and now their lot was up. However, the remaining Pinkerton detective had an ace up his sleeve: a small hidden pistol the outlaws hadn't found. It was now or never. He whipped out the hidden gun and put a bullet through John's neck. As John lurched in his saddle, he gave the Pinkerton both barrels of his shotgun, shredding the man's arm. Jim shot the deputy sheriff right off his horse, killing him instantly.

The Pinkerton, in agony from his mutilated arm, wheeled his horse and galloped away with John riding right after him, blood pouring from the wound in his neck. Though he was mortally wounded, John managed to draw a pistol and shoot the Pinkerton in the back. Then darkness set in and both men slipped from the saddle, dead.

This chain of events and the death of Archie Samuel was a public relations nightmare for Pinkerton. They had failed to capture Jesse and Frank James (in spite of the early reports, the brothers had been tipped off and weren't at the house that night), and a little boy had been blown up. The Missouri legislature was demanding an investigation, and public opinion, which had been on the side of Pinkerton and his detectives, shifted. Almost overnight, the Pinkertons came to be seen by the public as a group of ruthless thugs who had no problem working outside the law. Pinkerton's desire to get revenge on the James brothers permanently lowered the reputation of his detectives.

The pursuit of Frank and Jesse James was the last case Allan Pinkerton was involved in concerning the pursuit of outlaws. Private companies no longer hired him to go after gangs of thieves, as such work was left to local police and U.S. Marshals on the frontier. As for the James-Younger gang, they would infamously be done in after a bank robbery in Northfield, Minnesota went haywire, resulting in town citizens fighting it out in the streets and wounding and killing several of the robbers.

Much has been made of the incident at Northfield, Minnesota that resulted in the demise of the James-Younger Gang. For 15 years, they had terrorized parts of the West and the South, so it was unbelievable to some that a group of Minnesotans would be able to do what the law and the Pinkertons had not. Some speculate that the bandits must have been drunk. Others say that they lost the element of surprise and were too visible, creating suspicion. Perhaps it was simply because they underestimated their opponents. These were Civil War veterans and some had fought the Sioux in 1862. Most were deer hunters and knew how to use a gun. Whatever the reason, they did not back down when the former Confederates came into their town to try and take their hard-earned money.

In 1896, the Pinkertons were instrumental in disbanding Butch Cassidy, the Sundance Kid, and the Wild Bunch. The Wild Bunch is as much myth as it is fact, and they certainly never called themselves the Wild Bunch. In fact, it was not until the Pinkerton Detective Agency called them the Wild Bunch that anyone had ever heard the name. As many as 30 different men have been linked to the gang at various times, but very few of them committed more than one or two holdups with each other. It's also unclear how many crimes they were actually responsible for, or just how many Butch Cassidy and Sundance Kid actively participated in. It's altogether possible that Sundance had never even met Cassidy before he was released from jail in 1896, and only three heists can be linked back to them, but the gang's reputation would be firmly established, and Cassidy and Sundance would soon become two of the most wanted men in both North America and South America.

Butch Cassidy

The Sundance Kid

Though there is no evidence to suggest that Butch Cassidy was part of the Wilcox robbery, it seems likely that Sundance was there. A newspaper in Rawlins, Wyoming implicated three local bandits, but the Pinkertons were not at all convinced that this was not the work of the Wild Bunch. One of the descriptions matched that of Flat Nose, and the other two could have been Harvey Logan and his brother. Butch Cassidy had sworn to the governor of Wyoming that he would not commit any crimes there after he was given an early release from his prison sentence, and Cassidy was also not known to be violent, so the crime did not fit his modus operandi. When he saw his lawyer, William Simpson, days later and Simpson questioned him about the Wilcox robbery, Cassidy insisted he was not part of it.

That said, the Wild Bunch pooled the money from the various robberies, so it's likely Cassidy got a share of the money. It also helped the outlaws escape after their robberies. Even before conducting a robbery, Sundance and his fellow outlaws set up horse relays all along their escape route that allowed them to continue riding without having to rest their horses. They were well aware that a sheriff's posse was hot on their trail, so they stopped south of Hole-in-the-Wall near Lost Cabin to divvy up the money and go their separate ways, making it that much more difficult for the law to find them.

That posse, led by the sheriff of Converse County, Josiah Hazen, finally caught up with three of them on June 6 at Castle Creek, which was renamed Teapot Dome several years later. The area is a deep ravine with plenty of rocks for hiding, making Hazen a sitting duck when he rode right up toward Kid Curry, who shot and killed him in a gun battle. The rest of the posse hid while the outlaws got away.

Cassidy suggested going to Argentina to some of his Wild Bunch friends, but the only two who were interested in the plan were Kid Curry and Sundance. Kid Curry ultimately passed, but Sundance was in. On November 21, 1900, some members of the gang, including Sundance, Cassidy, and Kid Curry, had a last hurrah in Texas. They visited the red light districts to enjoy the liquor, the gambling, and the women. They also stopped in at John Swartz's photography studio and, dressed in their finest suits, had their photo taken. Swartz displayed the photo, which has been widely reproduced in the century since it was taken, on the window of his studio, having no idea that the five men he had photographed were wanted criminals. The photo found its way to the Pinkertons, who were grateful for the headshots to include on their wanted posters.

Sitting (L-R): Sundance Kid, Ben Kilpatrick (The Tall Texan), and Butch Cassidy

Standing (L-R): Will Carver (News Carver), and Harvey Logan (Kid Curry)

With operatives spread across North America and eventually South America, the Pinkertons had the ability to track the Wild Bunch when the trail went cold for law enforcement. Charlie Siringo, working under the alias Charles L. Carter on behalf of the Pinkertons, managed to infiltrate the Wild Bunch after the Wilcox robbery, and information obtained by Siringo put the heat on several members of the Wild Bunch. This resulted in the capture of Kid Curry, who was killed in a shootout in Colorado in 1904. Though not the most notorious of the gang, Kid Curry was the most feared, and it is believed he killed nearly 10 law enforcement officers in his short life. After he was captured in Tennessee, he headed to Montana and murdered a rancher who he claimed killed his brother years earlier. He was captured in Tennessee and escaped a second time, only to finally be killed in the Colorado shootout.

Cassidy and Sundance had split up after their excursion to Texas and planned to reconnect in New York on February 1, 1902, but Sundance did not arrive in the Big Apple alone. Sundance came east with the most mysterious of all the members of the Wild Bunch, a young woman best known today as Etta Place. The name and fate of Etta Place has remained one of the most enduring mysteries of the Butch and Sundance legend, and aside from the fact she was a long-time companion of Sundance's, little else is known about her. Whoever she was, Etta Place was using the maiden name of Sundance's mother (Annie Place), and she was referred to at times as Mrs. Harry Longabaugh or Mrs. Harry A. Place. She also once signed her name "Mrs. Ethel Place".

In fact, Etta Place is such a mystery that not even the Pinkertons knew if that was her real name. Since some have speculated that Etta was a music teacher, the connection is made back to Ethel Bishop, a music teacher in San Antonio. There are some who believe that Etta, who the Pinkertons called Ethel, was actually Ann Basset, but this was never confirmed. Although the pictures of Etta and Ann look strikingly alike, authorities strongly believe that Etta Place was with Sundance in South America from 1902-1904, while Ann was arrested for rustling cattle in Utah in 1903. Assuming she wasn't Ann Bassett, Etta Place was only one of five known women allowed in Robbers Roost, including the Bassett sisters, Elzy Lay's girlfriend Maude Davis, and gang member Laura Bullion.

The Pinkerton Agency's mugshot of Laura Bullion

There was speculation that Etta Place may have been Eunice Gray, who operated a house of ill repute in Fort Worth, but Gray never claimed to be Etta Place. A reporter simply speculated that after she said she had been in the Fort Worth area since 1901, aside from a brief trip to South America for a couple of years.

According to Donna Ernst, the Sundance Kid's biographer and niece, she looked at the records for every woman named Ethel born between 1875 and 1880 in San Antonio and Fort Worth, This was because, in addition to Etta, the Pinkertons referred to her as Ethel, Rita, and Eva Place. Ernst eliminated every woman named Ethel she uncovered in that timeframe other than Ethel Bishop, but this is still a stretch because there is no solid reason to believe that Etta Place's real first name is Etta. As for her place of birth, the Pinkertons believed it was Texas, as they had a lead suggesting that her parents were from there, but those that met Etta believed that she was from the East Coast.

Certainly, Etta exuded a certain sense of refinement in her speech and appearance. While in New York City, Sundance and Etta went to the DeYoung Photography Studio and had their portrait taken. Both looked like two of the city's most proper citizens, right down to the Tiffany watch that is pinned to Etta's dress. Neighbors that knew Etta and Sundance in South America recalled seeing Etta ride her horse English style, but despite her apparent cultured style, there were rumors that she was at one point in the employ of Ms. Fannie Porter of San Antonio, who ran one of the most upscale bordellos in all of the West. The Pinkertons interviewed her about what she might know about Etta Place, but she claimed ignorance. However, another of Porter's ladies did talk to the Pinkertons, and whatever she said led them to believe that Etta Place was once a prostitute there.

Sundance Kid and Etta Place before they headed to South America

What is known is that upon their arrival in New York City, Sundance and Etta presented themselves as Mr. and Mrs. Harry Place. Those that accept Etta Place as her real name conclude that she was Sundance's cousin, and it's been suggested that she was calling herself Etta Place because she and Sundance were married. Perhaps it signified nothing other than an alias for both of them. The Pinkertons said that the one photo that exists of the two was their wedding photo, but there are no records indicating that the two were married.

Before they made it to New York, Etta and Sundance rang in the New Year at New Orleans and then took a train to Pennsylvania to see Sundance's family in early 1901. Sundance introduced Etta to his sister and brothers as his wife and reportedly also told them that he wanted to go straight, which was the reason he was going to South America. He incorrectly presumed he would be away from the watchful eyes of the Pinkertons outside of the country.

The fact that Etta was with Butch Cassidy and Sundance strengthens the argument that they were not planning any more escapades in South America. Cassidy did not like having women around when they were planning a job, presumably because of the distraction they presented to the men.

If Cassidy and Sundance thought moving south of the border was going to shake the Pinkertons from their tails, they were mistaken. The Pinkertons knew that they were with Etta Place in Buenos Aires, and in July 1903 the chief of the Buenos Aires police force received a letter from Robert Pinkerton. He advised him that the bandits were in their vicinity and included the most recent photographs that the agency had on file, as well as descriptions. The Pinkertons had operatives in South America and asked an agent in Argentina to go to their ranch and arrest them, but the operative said it would have to wait. It was the rainy season and he could not easily travel inland, but the police chief did agree to monitor the three in case they tried to leave Argentina.

Much to the frustration of the Pinkertons, they would later come to find out that Etta and Sundance were right under their nose at one point. The two of them had returned to New York City on the *Soldier Prince* and arrived on April 3, 1902, signing in at a boarding house on the Lower East Side as Mr. and Mrs. Harry Place. Among their excursions was a trip to Coney Island, a trip to Atlantic City to meet up with Sundance's brother Harvey, and a trip to Pennsylvania, presumably to visit his sister. They may have also made their way to Chicago for Sundance to get treated for an old gunshot wound to his leg. Before leaving on the return trip to Argentina, they made another stop at Tiffany's and purchased a watch for $15.35. They did not leave until July, meaning that they had been in the U.S. for three months without being detected by the Pinkertons.

Whatever the circumstances, Cassidy, Sundance, and Etta lived a life of relative peace until the spring of 1906. It is not clear if they heard that the Pinkertons were going to make a move or if they simply got the urge to resume their criminal ways, but with Etta calmly holding the horses, an American fugitive helped Cassidy and Sundance rob a bank in Mercedes of $20,000. One of the three men killed the banker in the process before they split the proceeds and went their separate ways.

When the local newspaper ran a story about the robbery along with photos of Butch and Sundance, including a mention that the robbers spoke English, they were also suspected of a robbery in Rio Gallegos. That robbery set off reports that they were also involved in other robberies throughout South America, including banks at Bahia Blanca and a payroll train at Eucalyptus. They were even accused of killing a man in Arroyo Pescado in 1910, but this seems unlikely because murder was not their style, and, more importantly, it is highly likely that they were dead by then. Regardless of their actual involvement, the aftermath of the bank robbery at Mercedes meant Cassidy and Sundance were on the run again.

In the meantime, what became of Etta Place is a mystery. The last written record of her is at Arroyo Pescado, and then she disappeared from the records, despite the fact that the Pinkerton agency was supposedly keeping close tabs on her. Some historians believe she died in South America too, but a woman matching her physical description tried to get documentation legally declaring Harry Longabaugh dead in 1909. After that request was denied, that was the last the public saw or heard from Etta Place.

Of course, there were also many in law enforcement that had given up on the idea of catching Cassidy and Sundance as well, since they always seemed to be a step ahead of the people that were chasing them. However, their luck would seemingly run out in late 1908. Earlier in that year, the payroll for the Aramayo mines, located in the southern region of Bolivia, was robbed. That is a fact, but what happened after that is up for debate. Most historians agree that Cassidy and Sundance made their way to San Vicente on November 6. The local justice, known as the corregidor, made arrangements for them to stay in a spare room at the home of a local villager. Some say that it was a mule that gave them away to the corregidor. Cassidy and Sundance had taken the equipment off of their horses and mules, setting it all aside and letting the animals graze. Supposedly, the corregidor watched one of the mules roll on its back in the dust and recognized it as an animal that belonged to his friend. The mule had been used to transport the payroll to the Aramayo mines. He was suspicious, but also found the casual manner of Cassidy and Sundance to be unusual if they were, indeed, responsible for the robbery.

He alerted four members of the Bolivian cavalry, including a captain, that the Aramayo mine bandits may be in town. Soon after that, one of the soldiers entered a room where Cassidy and Sundance were staying – some say that they were fueling up on food and whiskey – but he was met by Cassidy, who shot and killed him. If true, this is believed to be the only man Cassidy ever killed. The other two men took cover and fired into the room. In the mean time, the captain instructed the corregidor to round up men from the village to surround the building to keep Cassidy and Sundance from escaping.

There are different versions of what may have happened next. There are reports that Sundance ran out onto the patio, shooting as he went, hoping to reach the rifles that were leaning along a wall. He was shot before he reached the end of the courtyard. Cassidy ran out to get him, taking more than one bullet himself, and dragged the mortally wounded Sundance back inside. There are also reports that shortly after the captain arrived, three loud screams were heard coming from the building, followed by silence.

The Bolivian army reported that when they finally entered the room they found the men believed to be Butch and Sundance dead. Sundance's body had several gunshot wounds to the arms and one to the forehead, while Cassidy had a wound to an arm and had also been shot in the temple. The Bolivians concluded that Cassidy put Sundance out of his misery before turning the gun on himself because they were out of ammunition. However, there are also reports that they had plenty of ammunition and Sundance even had a rifle nearby. The outlaws did have the money from the Aramayo mine, as well as map of Bolivia, and the payroll officer confirmed that the dead men were the same men that committed the robbery. An inquest was held, but Bolivian officials never officially identified the names of the dead bandits, who were quickly buried in the San Vicente cemetery.

Reports soon got back to friends of Cassidy and Sundance in Bolivia that they had died in San Vicente, and the last reported sighting of them was at the Hotel Terminus in Tupiza. A friend greeted Cassidy as Mr. Maxwell, one of his aliases, but Cassidy reportedly said that he was now going by Santiago Lowe. A man by that name was, indeed, a guest of the hotel that night. None of the newspaper articles about the incident ever referred to the outlaws by name, nor did they speculate that the famous Butch Cassidy and Sundance Kid had met their demise in the gun battle.

Nobody knows for sure why Butch Cassidy and the Sundance Kid went back to being criminals, but what is certain is that there are many people who hope they did not die in Bolivia and that instead, two of America's favorite bandits got a chance to live their final years in peace. Despite the fact that Butch and Sundance were criminals, the glimpses of their character that come through in stories about their lives demonstrate that they had the kind of swagger, charm, courage, and ability (or luck) to escape the law that Americans have come to associate with so many legends of the West. The same traits that made them two of the West's most successful outlaws will also ensure that Butch and Sundance continue to be two of the most romanticized figures of that era. It also helps explain why the Pinkertons were often reviled for their work.

Labor

Pinkerton's agency may have left the West behind, but back closer to home, there was still a market for his services. As labor unions, some of them engaged in violence to further their goals, grew in the United States, companies turned to the Pinkertons to infiltrate and disrupt their activities. This had the effect, ultimately, of further lowering the Pinkertons in the eyes of the general public, as they came to be seen as the tools of capital against labor. It was ironic, considering Pinkerton's youthful radicalism, that near the end of his life he would ally against the very class he came from.

The first anti-labor case Pinkerton and his men worked was against the Molly Maguires. The "Mollies," as they were commonly known, were purported to be a secret organization that began in Ireland in the early 19th century targeting British authorities in rural areas. Most of the activities involved targeting the enclosure of formerly small plots of land into large estates run by absentee landlords. This included such things as the destruction of fences, but also attacks on the managers of the larger estates. It is believed that the Molly Maguires came to America with

Irish immigrants and settled in the anthracite coal region of Pennsylvania, including the counties of Lackawanna, Luzerne, Columbia, Schuylkill, Carbon, and Northumberland. They brought the same violent techniques used in Ireland in confronting the owners of the coal mines.

Horrible working conditions and economic hardships caused low pay to drive thousands of miners to unionize. The Workingman's Benevolent Association (WBA) gained some 20,000 members in 1869 in the aftermath of a mine disaster at the Avondale Mine in Luzerne county. The WBA was committed to peaceful action, but the mine owners conflated the union with the Molly Maguires, primarily in an attempt to discredit the former by citing the violence of the latter. Unrest and union activity in the coal areas accelerated by the time of the Panic of 1873, which caused high unemployment among the coal miners. Fear of more violence led the mine owners to seek action against the Molly Maguires.

In 1873, Pinkerton was contacted by Franklin B. Gowen, president of the Philadelphia and Reading Railroad and of the Philadelphia and Reading Coal and Iron Company. Considered "the wealthiest anthracite coal mine owner in the world," Gowan had had enough of the Mollies and the threat be believe they posed to his mines. Robert A Pinkerton, the son of Allan Pinkerton, explained in a letter, "It was owing to Mr. Gowen....that the Molly Maguire organization was broken up. Mr. Gowen, when a young man, had been District Attorney of Schuylkill County, and, while occupying this office, had found great difficulty in convicting men accused of crimes, as the Mollys would swear to alibis for any of their members arrested. When he afterwards became the president of the Philadelphia and Reading Railroad, in order to protect its interests, and its employees, and the managers and superintendents of the mines which it he found it necessary to break up this organization, and it was then he consulted Mr. Allan Pinkerton."

Gowen

Pinkerton assigned James McParland for the task. A native of County Armagh, Ireland, McParland was evidently a particular favorite of Pinkerton's. Pinkerton's obituary even mentioned him: "He [Pinkerton] was a man who detected at once what qualities there were in a person that came under his observation. A striking illustration of this fact is the career of McParlan. the great detective in the Molly Maguire cases. McParlan was a coachman in the employ of a merchant who resides in Chicago. The stables of this gentleman joined those of Pinkerton on Monroe street, and 'the old man,' then deeply involved in the study of the Molly Maguire cases, came to the conclusion that 'Mac' was his man. He engaged him at a high salary, instructed him personally for hours every day, and finally turned him over to the agency, which had the special management of this great case."

McParland took the alias of James McKenna and went undercover against the Mollies. His assignment was to collect evidence of murder plots and other plans for violence against the mines and to pass the information on to his Pinkerton supervisor. He also worked with a Pinkerton agent assigned to the Coal and Iron Police to coordinate the eventual arrest and prosecution of members of the Molly Maguires. Pinkerton's instructions to McParland were straight and to the point. 'You are to remain in the field until every cut-throat has paid with his life for the lives so cruelly taken.'"

McParland established his headquarters at Shenandoah, but he did not find it easy at first to locate the Mollies, much less infiltrate them. As a later article published in *McClures Magazine* noted, "After some weeks of reconnoitering on foot through the coal regions, the young detective arrived in Pottsville, where he established himself in a boarding-house kept by a Mrs. O'Regan. There he met a man named Jennings, who volunteered to show him the sights of the city that same night. Passing a noisy drinking-place called the Sheridan House, McKenna, for that was McParland's assumed name, proposed going in. Jennings warned him as he valued his life never to cross the threshold of that place. 'It's kept by Pat Dormer,' he said, 'the big body-master of the Molly Maguires. He stands six feet four, weighs two hundred and fifty pounds, and is a bad man.'"

After giving his skittish companion the slip, McParland made his way back to the saloon. Ingratiating himself to all assembled by buying a round of drinks, he was invited to a game of cards. McParland, who was partnered with Dormer in the game, found out that one of the men playing, who was a notoriously boastful bully, was cheating. "The result was a fight in the handball alley, which Pat Dormer lighted up especially for the purpose, the company of Mollys ranging themselves in an appreciative circle to see Frazer demolish the plucky little fellow, who, though strong and agile, was far out-classed in height and I weight. In the first round Frazer caught the detective a swinging right-harder under the ear and knocked him down, while the spectators applauded. But the battle was not over yet; for McKenna's blood was up, and he was a hard hitter, his arm being nerved by the consciousness that much depended upon his victory. Six times in succession he floored the bully of Pottsville, and the seventh time Frazer fell heavily on his face and failed to get up again."

This action ingratiated McParland to the Mollies, and he became well established in their ranks. He soon established that the members of the Molly Maguires were also members of a benevolent society, the Ancient Order of Hibernians.

As McParland gathered information concerning the Mollies, the coal operators decided to ratchet up pressure on the coal miners with the goal of exterminating the Molly Maguires and breaking the labor unions. In December 1874, Gowen persuaded the other coal operators to announce a 20% pay cut, using the economic slowdown as an excuse. In response, the miners decided to strike on January 1, 1875. There were outbreaks of violence as a result, and ironically, most of the violence was targeted at the miners by representatives of the mining companies. For example, Edward Coyle, one of the union leaders, was murdered in March. A mine boss by the name of Patrick Vary fired into a group of miners, and another meeting of miners was attacked at Tuscarora, leaving one killed and several others wounded.

Influenced by the information received from McParland and Robert Linden, another Pinkerton agent assigned to the Coal and Iron Police, Pinkerton came to believe that the Mollies required a more direct - and extralegal - approach. In an August 29, 1875 letter to his general superintendent, Pinkerton recommended vigilante action against the Molly Maguires, telling him, "The M.M.'s are a species of Thugs... Let Linden get up a vigilance committee. It will not do to get many men, but let him get those who are prepared to take fearful revenge on the M.M.'s. I think it would open the eyes of all the people and then the M.M.'s would meet with their just deserts."

On December 10, 1875, three men and two women were attacked at home by masked men. The victims, as it turned out, had been identified by McParland as members of the Molly Maguires. One of the men was killed in the house, two other men were wounded but able to escape, and the wife of one of the reputed members of the Molly Maguires was shot dead.

The attack outraged McParland. When he heard the details of the attack, he wrote a letter of protest to his Pinkerton supervisor:

> "Friday: This morning at 8 A.M. I heard that a crowd of masked men had
> entered Mrs. O'Donnell's house ... and had killed James O'Donnell alias Friday,
> Charles O'Donnell and James McAllister, also Mrs. McAllister whom they took
> out of the house and shot ... Now as for the O'Donnells I am satisfied they got
> their just deserving. I reported what those men were. I give all information about
> them so clear that the courts could have taken hold of their case at any time but
> the witnesses were too cowardly to do it. I have also in the interests of God and
> humanity notified you months before some of those outrages were committed still
> the authorities took no hold of the matter. Now I wake up this morning to find that
> I am the murderer of Mrs. McAllister. What had a woman to do with the case—
> did the [Molly Maguires] in their worst time shoot down women. If I was not here
> the Vigilante Committee would not know who was guilty and when I find them
> shooting women in their thirst for blood I hereby tender my resignation to take

effect as soon as this message is received. It is not cowardice that makes me resign but just let them have it now I will no longer interfere as I see that one is the same as the other and I am not going to be an accessory to the murder of women and children. I am sure the [Molly Maguires] will not spare the women so long as the Vigilante has shown an example."

In response to McParland's belief that his daily reports had been made available to the vigilantes, his supervisor Benjamin Franklin assured him that "the Pinkerton agency has nothing to do with the vigilante murders. McParland was persuaded not to resign, and he continued his work against the Mollies.

The strike was broken by June 1875 through the imprisonment of the strike leaders and violence directed at the miners. Miners returned to work, accepting the 20 % cut, but miners associated with the Molly Maguires continued their campaign, and there were more incidents of violence as support for the Mollies increased. McParland reported, "Men, who last winter would not notice a Molly Maguire, are now glad to take them by the hand and make much of them. If the bosses exercise tyranny over the men they appear to look to the association for help." He also reported an increasing cycle of violence between the Mollies and the mine owners: "November was a bloody month what with the miners on strike.... In the three days around November 18, a Mollie was found dead in the streets of Carbondale, north of Scranton, a man had his throat cut, an unidentified man was crucified in the woods, a mining boss mauled, a man murdered in Scranton, and three men of [another Molly Maguires group] were guilty of a horror against an old woman, and an attempt to assassinate a Mollie by the name of Dougherty, followed and [Dougherty] at once demanded the murder of W. M. Thomas, whom he blamed for the attempt.""

McParland mentioned numerous plots of the Mollies to attack mine superintendents and guards and destroy property, including an aborted plan to destroy a railroad bridge, and ultimately, his reports formed that basis for trials of members of the Molly Maguires. Gowen, who had kickstarted the Pinkerton investigation of the Mollies, had himself appointed as special prosecutor.

McParland's testimony in the Molly Maguires trials was key to obtaining guilty verdicts. Gowen, during the trial of several Molly Maguires, addressed the role of McParlen's testimony:

"The Commonwealth propose to prove by the witness, James McParlan, that as a detective officer he became a member of an organization known as the Ancient Order of Hibernians, of which each one of the defendants on trial was a member, together with Hurley and Doyle; that as a member of that organization, he, the witness, became cognizant of the fact that the organization was criminal in its character ; that the attack made upon William M. Thomas was made in pursuance of a confederation among all the prisoners now on trial and others, as members of that order, and acting as such ; and that the attack and wounding of William M. Thomas was made by certain of the prisoners now on trial, in pursuance of the agreement or confederation before referred to. This to be followed by proof of the attack upon and wounding of William M. Thomas.

"We further propose to prove by the witness the rules, purpose, and character of the organization, and all the circumstances connected with the confederacy or conspiracy to kill William M. Thomas. It is proposed to prove that the attack upon and wounding of William M. Thomas was made in pursuance of the rules, regulations, and orders of this association, with the knowledge, co-operation, and connivance of all the prisoners now on trial."

Speaking of the impact of his testimony, the Canton, Ohio *Stark County Democrat* wrote, "Ever since James McParlen, the Pinkerton detective, made his disclosures upon the witness stand of the horrible fact that there had existed for a number or years in the Anthracite coal region an oath-bound society, whose ostensible object was a good and beneficial one, but whose real object had been to obtain control of the industrial and political interests of that region by threats of violence which they showed themselves both willing and able to carry into effect, this community has felt that the punishment for the crimes committed by them was a matter upon which the very existence of their lives and properties of the citizens depended."

As a result of the trials, ten Molly Maguires were executed, breaking the back of the organization and establishing the Pinkertons' reputation as the defenders of corporations and business owners against workers and their attempt to organize labor unions. Over the next 20 years, the Pinkertons became involved in several labor management disputes, including the infamous Homestead Steel strike in which several Pinkerton agents were killed and others were forced to surrender to strikers after an armed standoff. That strike led to the passage of the Anti-Pinkerton Act of 1893, which prohibited the federal government from hiring private investigative agencies. Several states passed similar laws.

As for the man who started it all, Allen Pinkerton died in Chicago on July 1, 1884, and the circumstances surrounding his death are somewhat confused. As he grew older, he developed several illnesses, including flare-ups of the malaria that he contracted during his mission through the South during the Civil War. When he was 65, he suffered a mild stroke. But the most widely accepted story is the strangest. One day, while Pinkerton was out walking his wife's poodle, the dog wrapped its leash around his legs. Pinkerton tripped, fell to the concrete, and bit his own tongue. The tongue became infected and developed gangrene. He died a few days later.

Newspapers around the country published laudatory obituaries, conveniently glossing over some of the more notorious incidents. Of his career, the Washington, D.C. *Evening Star* wrote, "Allan Pinkerton was a man who knew no fear, and numerous are the exploits in which he took his life in his own hands. On one occasion, in Detroit, he was so severely handled by his adversaries that his life was despaired of. A partial lameness remained to the last as the result of the bloody encounter. He was a man who a detected at once what qualities there were in a person that came under his observation… Mr. Pinkerton was the author of fifteen volumes of detective experiences. He has left several volumes in manuscript. He never could be induced to operate in a divorce case or where family matters were in dispute."

The *Donaldsonville Chief* told readers, "In prosecuting his business Mr. Pinkerton made it his inflexible rule never to operate for reward or on payments contingent upon success, and would never allow any of his operatives to receive any reward or gratuity for their success. He paid his employes liberally, and worked for those who engaged him at a certain fixed sum per diem, which was all that was ever received. Another noticeable feature of the nature of his immense business, and one of the strictest rules of his institution, was that he never under any circumstances could be induced to operate in a divorce case, or where family matters were in dispute."

The plaque at his tomb in Chicago shows how Pinkerton wanted to be remembered:

A Friend to Honesty

And a foe to crime

Devoting himself for a generation to the prevention and detection of crime in many countries, he was the founder in America of a noble profession. In the hour of the nation's peril, he conducted Abraham Lincoln safely through the ranks of treason to the scene of his first inauguration as President. He sympathized with, protected and defended the slaves, and labored earnestly for their freedom. Hating wrong, and loving good, he was strong, brave, tender and true.

The Pinkerton National Detective Agency outlived its founder. Pinkerton's two sons, Robert and William, took over the operation of the agency. Under their leadership, the agency continued to grow, to the extent that by the 1890s, it employed 2,000 active agents and 30,000 reserves.

In addition to countering the Wild Bunch in that decade, The Pinkertons continued to be employed by corporations against labor union activities. Despite the Homestead debacle, they were hired by companies to break strikes in Illinois, West Virginia, Michigan, New York, and Pennsylvania. They continued to be closely associated with strikebreaking until the La Follette Committee hearings in 1937 cast a sharp light on the Agency's anti-labor practices. Under the leadership of Allan Pinkerton's great-grandson, Robert Pinkerton II, the Pinkertons ended the anti-labor activities and criminal investigative activities. The agency re-oriented to personal and corporate security, taking on high-profile clients around the world.

One of the Pinkerton Agency's most notable protection assignments did not involve a person, though it did involve one of the most famous faces in history. In 1968, the agency was hired to escort the Mona Lisa on its voyage from the United States, where it had been on display in the National Gallery of Art in Washington and the Metropolitan Museum of Art in New York City. As the Pinkerton advertising stated, "The priceless painting played to record crowds on this side of the Atlantic. Now she had to be escorted home…safely. This was a job for Pinkerton's. Two armed investigators kept a constant vigil all during the return voyage. There were no incidents. That's how it usually goes when Pinkerton's is there. After all, Pinkerton's has been the largest, most effective security organization in the U.S. for 118 years."

In 1999, Securitas AB, the largest security services provider in the world, acquired Pinkerton. They still operate under the name of their founder, operating in the 21st century and offering an array of security and risk management services to clients around the world.

THE LATE ALLAN PINKERTON.

A depiction of Pinkerton in 1884

Pinkerton's tomb

Online Resources

Other books about 19th century American history by Charles River Editors

Other books about Pinkerton on Amazon

Further Reading

Seiple, Samantha (October 2015). Lincoln's Spymaster: Allan Pinkerton, America's First Private Eye. New York: Scholastic Press.

Horan, James D. (1969) [First published 1967]. The Pinkertons: The Detective Dynasty That Made History. New York, USA: Crown Publishers.

Mackay, James (1996). Allan Pinkerton: The First Private Eye. New York: John Wiley and Sons.

Free Books by Charles River Editors

We have brand new titles available for free most days of the week. To see which of our titles are currently free, click on this link.

Discounted Books by Charles River Editors

We have titles at a discount price of just 99 cents everyday. To see which of our titles are currently 99 cents, click on this link.